THE VERMONT CHEESE BOOK

THE VERMONT CHEESE BOOK

Ellen Ecker Ogden

THE COUNTRYMAN PRESS
WOODSTOCK, VERMONT

This book is dedicated to my devoted border collie Robin, who loved the farm life.
In Memorium 1992–2006

ISBN 978-0-88150-770-6

Cover and insert photos by Andrew Wellman
Cheese diagrams in color insert by Kelly Thompson
Interior photos by the author, except where noted
Book design and composition by Eugenie S. Delaney
Maps by Jacques Chazaud

Published by The Countryman Press,
P.O. Box 748, Woodstock, Vermont 05091

Distributed by W. W. Norton & Company, Inc.,
500 Fifth Ave., New York, NY 10110

Printed in the United States of America

10 9 8 7 6 5 4 3 2 1

ON THE COVER: *The Vermont state flower, the red clover, symbolizes the diversity of the wild flora that thrives in the state's healthy soil, which in turn nourishes the animals and is ultimately reflected in the flavor of Vermont cheese. Also featured are two soft-ripened cheeses made at Lazy Lady Farm: Les Pyramids (right) and Demi-Tasse.*

FRONTISPIECE: *Farmer/cheesemaker Janine Putnam communes with contented Jersey cows in the lush hillside pastures of Thistle Hill Farm. Photo courtesy of Thistle Hill Farm*

ACKNOWLEDGMENTS

MY SINCERE THANKS GO to many people who helped with this book, but first and foremost to all the members of the Vermont Cheese Council, a trade organization dedicated to the production and advancement of Vermont cheese. It was the council's guide, *The Vermont Cheese Trail*, that led me to discover the diversity of farms and cheeses all over the state.

I give my deep appreciation to so many who went out of their way to be helpful to me: Angela Miller, my agent, who shared her enthusiasm and knowledge about cheese; Andrew Wellman for capturing distinctive color images of Vermont cheeses; Lauryn Axelrod, who helped me sustain a writing tempo that kept in time with my deadlines; Pam Knights and her husband, Chef Peter Heaney, for their friendship and hospitality during my travels along the northern routes; wine consultant Daphne Amory for her expert beverage pairing; and to the staff at Countryman Press who were at all times generous with advice and expertise. I am especially grateful to managing editor Jennifer Thompson for her vision and ability to bring together talented professionals, including book designer Eugenie Delaney and final copy editor Amy Rost. All helped me greatly in bringing this book to its final form.

On the home front, my appreciation will always go to friends Dagny St. John, who inspires me everyday with her adventurous spirit, and Peter Moore, whose zeal to taste a new Vermont cheese never failed to keep me going. With all my heart, I especially acknowledge my children, Molly and Sam, for their love and support and who understand firsthand the joys of a family farm.

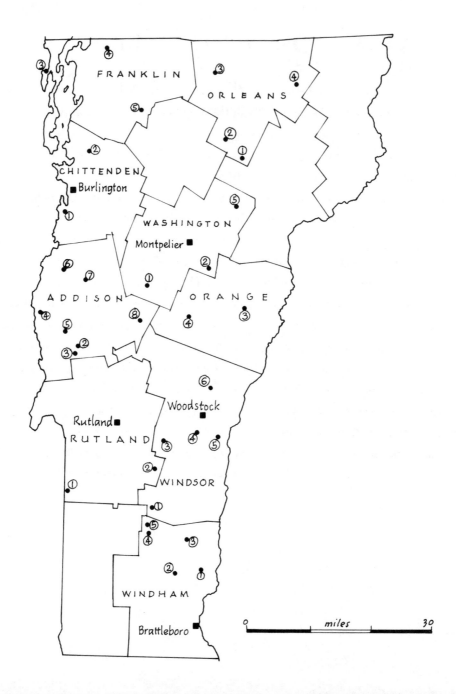

FRANKLIN

ORLEANS

CHITTENDEN

■ Burlington

WASHINGTON

Montpelier ■

ADDISON

ORANGE

Woodstock ■

Rutland ■

RUTLAND

WINDSOR

WINDHAM

Brattleboro ■

0   miles   30

CONTENTS

ABOUT THIS BOOK

*D*URING THE SUMMER OF 2006, I followed a map published by the Vermont Cheese Council to visit thirty-three cheesemakers in every corner in the state. My goal was to observe the landscape that surrounded the farms, observe farmers as they rotated animals into verdant pastures, and watch each cheesemaker in his or her make room (where the cheese is made) while culture was stirred into the warm milk or fresh curds hand-pressed into cheese molds. I quickly discovered that while there are similar methods to the art of cheesemaking, each farm had its own style, right down to the way it aged cheese.

The story behind every Vermont cheese goes beyond the beautiful label, the high-quality milk, the professional techniques, and the microflora that permeates the natural rinds of the cave-ripened cheese. Each farm and company has history. *The Vermont Cheese Book* takes you on a culinary journey through the colorful landscape of Vermont to explore the geography, the diversity of the farms, and the flavors of the cheese. Whether you are exploring the state's back roads by car or by bike, or simply enjoying the essence of Vermont cheese, this book will enhance your experience.

ABOUT THE CHEESE DESCRIPTIONS

Each of the farms and companies in *The Vermont Cheese Book* are members of the Vermont Cheese Council, and more information about the farms can be found on the council's Web site: www.vtcheese.com. While I was fortunate to savor many of the excellent cheeses featured in this book, it is not my intention to review or rate each company's products. In the interests of accuracy, many of the descriptions have been adapted from the farm or cheese company brochures and Web sites. As is the case with any handcrafted product, there will be variations from season to season, and types of cheese offered by each farm will continue to evolve.

INTRODUCTION

T WAS THE SPRING OF 2002 when I first met Henry Tewksbury, standing in front of the cheese counter at the Brattleboro Food Co-op. He was seventy-nine, wearing his signature Greek fisherman's hat and a formal, striped dress shirt tucked into dark blue jeans. A crisp, white, double-breasted chef's jacket protected his attire, but by noon the jacket was no longer looking fresh. Velcro sneakers gave away the truth about his job—he rarely sat down.

Tewksbury's book, *The Cheeses of Vermont* (The Countryman Press, 2002), and the growing popularity of artisan and farmstead cheese put him in the limelight as both a local and a national authority. Known affectionately as "Henry the Cheeseman," he was the man to talk to if you loved cheese.

Holding a plastic-wrapped wedge of creamy, yellow Brie, the interior oozing out along the edges of its tidy triangular form, he sang with approval, "Now this is a truly deliciously ripe cheese!" He turned it over in his hands, admiring it. "But most people would look at this and think it was way beyond its prime. Cheese is alive and it tastes better the older it gets. And this one is just getting started!"

Tewksbury knew that nothing sells cheese like a taste of it, and on the day I visited with him at the cheese counter, he proved his point. A man approached with a shopping basket containing two bottles of red wine that he was buying for a dinner party. He picked up the ripening Brie, studying it for a moment before Tewksbury said, "Would you like to taste it?" Tewksbury knew that no amount of sniffing through plastic wrap could top a message sent directly to the palate.

"If I see someone trying to decide what to buy, I always ask if they would like to taste a sample," he said, winking at me as the customer beamed, then carefully placed the wedge of cheese in his basket. "How else are they ever going to know what they like?"

He guided me to a six-foot-long cooler that held only Vermont-made cheeses. Rounds of soft Camembert, Brie, and chèvre sat alongside chunks of harder cheese, such as cheddar, Colby, and Gouda, all artfully displayed in baskets lined with colorful cloth napkins. Tiny baskets of cheese cubes with "taste me" signs were nestled in between. The labels on the cheese—most featuring drawings of cows and goats—were each unique and handmade, like the product within.

"Let's get the vocabulary right," Tewksbury said. "Farmstead cheese is made on the farm where the animals are raised. Artisan cheese is handmade, but the milk is brought in from nearby farms. And then there is factory made, where no human hands touch the product."

The Vermont Cheese Council was established in 1997 and within a few years began to promote Vermont Cheese Week. The week-long series of events gave cheesemakers a chance to get off the farm and make personal appearances at food co-ops, specialty stores, and restaurants to talk about their products, share samples, and provide consumers with information about the farms. The Vermont Cheese Council still has an active membership, and members continue to band together for educational and tasting events throughout the state. During the mid-1990s, when artisan and farmstead cheesemakers were under pressure from lawmakers who wanted to regulate the production of raw-milk cheese, Tewksbury and others crusaded against legislation requiring that all cheeses be pasteurized. Tewksbury told me that pasteurization laws were born of an age when they were needed, when small cheesemaking operations were far from sterile.

"But it is not true anymore," he said. He had visited Vermont farms as research for his book and confirmed that today each operation is impeccably clean. "The best cheese is alive with bacteria, and pasteurization will knock 50 percent of the flavor out of the cheese." Moreover, the current state mandate says raw-milk cheese must be held for sixty days before it can be sold. "When cheese is aged for more than two months, it is automatically pasteurized," he said.

Making cheese is a Vermont tradition. Two hundred years ago, every farm had an average of a dozen cows and made their own butter and cheese. During the mid-1800s, farmers brought their milk to cheese co-ops—centrally located, commercial cheesemaking factories. These co-ops turned milk into butter and cheese, primarily Cheddar, as a way to preserve milk that would otherwise spoil. (At that time, chunks of ice were the only form of refrigeration available.)

Today, only a few of the original cheesemakers, such as Crowley Cheese (established in 1824), Grafton Cheese Company (established in 1892), and Cabot Creamery (established in 1893) remain. But cheesemaking has again become a farmhouse activity, and farmstead and artisan cheesemaking is experiencing a revival in Vermont.

Since Tewksbury's book was published in 2002, the state has developed an unexpectedly robust cheese industry. Thanks to Tewksbury, Professor Paul Kinstedt at the University of Vermont, cheesemaker and instructor Peter Dixon, and the members of the Vermont Cheese Council, the traditions and the art of cheesemaking are being revitalized, and with this return to cheesemaking has come a revival of the state's family farms.

Sadly, Tewksbury passed away in the spring of 2003, but his expertise and enthusiasm for cheese had fueled my own interest. As a food writer and organic gardener, I was curious to see how today's farmers cultivated their passion for agriculture, while producing cheese that brought so much culinary pleasure to the table.

Making cheese is a basic formula, but Vermont farmers are proving that it requires more than a recipe. It requires nurturing both the soil and the flock or herd and a healthy respect for the process of turning raw milk into cheese. Behind every soft-ripened, gently seasoned wedge and every wheel of naturally aged Vermont cheese is a passionate cheesemaker and a farm committed to healthy farming practices and respect for the animals. Vermont cheesemakers have made a commitment to a lifestyle, and the result is award-winning cheese that reflects tradition, dedication, and a sense of place.

Tasting cheese on the farm is quite a different experience than tasting it in a store, a restaurant, or standing at your kitchen counter. The smell of the animals in the barn, the view of verdant fields, and sight of farmers moving fences for crop rotation or tenderly ushering their animals into milking stalls—these are the special ingredients that make Vermont cheese so exceptional.

CHEESEMAKING BASICS

The story of any cheese starts with milk. The first two questions that a cheesemaker considers when embarking on the cheesemaking process are what type of milk to use, and whether the milk is raw (unpasteurized) or pasteurized.

Vermont cheese is currently made of milk from cows, sheep, goats, and water buffaloes —all cloven-hoofed mammals belonging to the biological family classification *Bovidea* and further classified as ruminants. The protein and butterfat content in the milk varies from species to species; it also dictates the type of cheese that can be made from the milk and the cheese's ultimate flavor and texture. Pasteurized milk has been heated to destroy harmful organisms. But because heating also robs the milk of some of its natural enzymes and flavor, many cheesemakers use unpasteurized, or raw, milk.

The third question a cheesemaker asks is how milk fits together with the other three primary ingredients: starter, rennet, and salt. Answering this question takes experimenting with recipes. Because the chemistry of the milk changes with the time of the year and what the animals are eating, the same recipe doesn't always work out the same way.

Milk is an extremely complex, highly perishable biological material, and successfully handling and processing milk requires a thorough understanding of its properties. Farmers and cheesemakers need to know the composition of the milk they are working with from a scientific perspective, as well as how the time of year will affect the butterfat and protein content. Animals eat different foods at different times of the year, and what the animals eat affects the flavor of their milk and, ultimately, the cheese. Young, fresh goat-milk cheese, for instance, is best made in spring and early summer, as the goats feed in the lush pastures full of wild herbs and flowers. Aged cheese, such as blue cheese or a natural-rind tomme, is made from summer milk and will be at its peak during the winter.

Other factors—such as how much fat is retained in the milk, moisture level, the type of rennet, the type of cultures added during the cheesemaking process and during the affinage (the last step in the cheesemaking process), and how long and where the cheese matures—are also crucial to the character of the cheese. These elements can make an apparently identical cheese from one producer taste completely different from the cheese of another.

HOW CHEESE IS MADE: STEP BY STEP

Each cheesemaker has his or her own method, which they often practice with myriad times before getting a satisfactory result. From the moment the milk is collected, however, all cheesemaking follows the same basic steps.

Step 1: Milk

Farmstead cheese is made from milk pumped directly from the barn to vats in the cheese room, while artisan cheese is made from milk delivered from or picked up at another farm. Some cheesemakers collect milk for a day or two, keeping it cool until they're

STEP 1 AND STEP 2: *Shepherd/cheesemaker Neil Urie and his assistant, Maria Shuman, of Bonnieview Farm in Craftsbury Common demonstrate how to make Ben Nevis, a sheep's milk cheese. First, the milk is heated with a starter culture, which acidifies the milk and converts the lactose to lactic acid. Then rennet is added, which coagulates the liquid. Here, Maria stirs the "set" milk, as the curds (solid matter) separate from the whey (the liquid).*

STEP 3: *Neil Urie scoops curds out of the liquid whey.*

ready to make cheese once or twice a week. Others will make cheese every day from the fresh warm milk, which reduces the time it takes to reheat the milk and keeps the product fresh.

Every cheese has a little variation, which makes it unique, but the general method involves heating the milk slowly in steel or copper vats until it reaches approximately 90 degrees. Then a starter culture is added to sour the milk and lower the pH to the desired acidity level; the type of starter, too, varies depending on the type of cheese. The starter also converts the lactose to lactic acid.

Step 2: Rennet

After some time—anywhere from twenty minutes to up to two hours, depending on the cheese recipe—rennet is added. Authentic rennet comes from the lining of the fourth stomach of a calf, but today cheesemakers often use vegetable-based or synthetically produced rennet without affecting the cheese flavor. Either way, only a minute amount is necessary to start the coagulation process.

Once the rennet is stirred into the warm milk, it needs time to act—sometimes up to an hour. During this time, the vat is slowly heated and kept close to 90 degrees, and the milk "sets," or becomes custard-like in consistency. In some cases, such in making a washed-curd cheese such as Gouda or Colby, the curds are rinsed with water.

Step 3: Cutting or Breaking the Curds

Once the milk is firm and springy to the touch, it is cut into small pieces with wire knives or a blade, which dice the firmed milk into small cubes. Cutting separates the curds from the watery residue, the whey. Both the curds and whey need to be handled delicately to keep the solids intact. The mixture is heated to 101 degrees to expel even more liquid.

Little of the original volume is left after this step. The basic ratio of raw milk to cheese will vary depending on the type of milk used. It takes approximately five pounds of sheep's milk or ten pounds of cow's milk to make one pound of cheese.

Step 4: Separating the Curds and Whey

The mixture is cooled, and the soft curds are transferred to cheese molds, while the whey is drained. When Cheddar is made, the drained curds are sliced into slabs and hand-fuls of salt are strewn over the top. The curds are then stacked to release even more whey.

The leftover whey can be to fed to

STEP 4: *The curds are poured into cheese molds.*

STEP 5: *Urie presses the curds to release more of the whey and to form into the domed-square shape distinctive of Ben Nevis.*

livestock—it is often used to fatten pigs—or used to fertilize gardens and fields.

Step 5: Pressing

Gently pressing the curds into the cheese molds releases the whey, in addition to forming the shape of the final cheese. The curds can be pressed by hand. Bonnieview Farm, for example, hand-presses the curds for its semisoft Ben Nevis cheese. Since Cheddar is typically aged for a minimum of two months, its curds are pressed between cheesecloth on a mechanical press or using weights. The cheese will stay in the molds anywhere from three hours to overnight, depending on the type of cheese.

Step 6: Salting and Curing

Once the cheese is removed from the molds, it will rest on shelves to allow the exterior to dry slightly. Then it is either waxed or dipped in a salty brine, which will help it form a natural rind.

Before transferring the cheese to a cool aging room, some cheesemakers may wash a natural rind with a liquid such as balsamic vinegar, beer, or brine, to encourage healthy mold spores to

STEP 6: *Removed from their molds, the shaped cheeses dry on shelves before being transferred to the aging room (above).*
STEP 7: *Once transferred to a cool aging room or cave, the cheese is left on oak shelves, where it will pick up microflora and be carefully turned, in a process known as affinage, to enhance a rich and mellow flavor (below).*

grow and heighten the character of the cheese. Soft-ripened cheeses, which develop rapidly, are sometimes misted with an inoculate that produces gentle white mold to ripen the cheese from the outside in.

Step 7: Aging and Affinage

Once it is transferred to a cool aging room, the cheese is left on oak shelves until its flavor is rich and mellow.

Affinage is the process of caring for the cheese and assisting in its full development. It can involve regularly turning the cheese to ensure that it ripens evenly, and often involves washing the outside of the cheese with brine, beer, balsamic vinegar or some other type of liquid for the first few weeks. The temperature of the aging cave, as well as the careful monitoring of the developing cheese, is tantamount to successful affinage.

MILK TYPE AND THE SEASONS

Most Vermont cheese is made from goat, cow, or sheep milk, and sometimes a combination of these. The type of milk used affects the flavor, texture, and character of a final product. All of the Vermont cheesemakers use fresh milk, which means the seasons greatly affect the flavor profile of the cheese. For example, the cheese made in the early spring, when the animals are grazing on fresh wild shoots, is typically redolent of flowers.

While it's difficult to generalize, here's a flavor profile of each type of milk to help guide you in your cheese selections and tasting.

Goat's Milk

Goats love to eat a variety of wild flora, including branches, leaves, brush, and in the summer months, flowers. Goat's milk contains less fat than that of a cow or sheep and tends to taste lighter and fresher. Fresh goat cheese is at its best from April to October. It is often described as complex, tangy, lemony, smooth, moist, and creamy, while goat's milk cheese that is made during the summer, then aged to be available in the winter, can take on a more intense, buttery, woodsy, and earthy essence.

Cow's Milk

It takes roughly ten gallons of cow's milk to make every one pound of cow's milk cheese. The fat content of the cheese will vary depending the type of cow's milk used. The milk of Jersey and Brown Swiss cows is known for its extra butterfat, while Ayrshire milk contains a specific fat globule that is ideal for certain types of cheese. Cows are more flexible in their breeding season, and different cows can be bred at different times so the cheesemaker has a steady supply of milk throughout the year. Typically, cow's milk cheese produced from April to October is a rich yellow-orange because it is full of natural carotenes; however, there are exceptions to this rule. Most cheesemakers include fresh hay in the cow's winter diet instead of fermented silage, which tends to produce bacteria and can result in a gas that forms in the cheese. Larger operations and those selling fresh cheese will pasteurize the milk, which eliminates the risk of bacteria. When cow's milk cheese is left unpasteurized and is naturally aged, it loses none of the natural enzymes which make it easy to digest, and its flavor often reflects the state of the pasture where the animals grazed.

Sheep's Milk

Sheep have a shorter milk-production season which—only five months long—much shorter than that of cows—so cheesemakers have only that long to capture milk for a cheesemaking season. Furthermore, the milk to cheese ratio is less than it is for either goats' or cows' milk; it takes five pounds of sheep's milk to make one pound of cheese. Lambing season in Vermont is usually timed for late spring, when the weather is warm enough for the animals to be outside comfortably. Sheep's milk cheeses are typically made right after lambing season; fresh soft ripened cheese will be ready in late spring, while wheels that are aged for several

UNPASTEURIZED VERSUS PASTEURIZED MILK

Vermont cheese is made in strict accordance to federal regulations for unpasteurized and pasteurized milk. Cheesemakers need to choose between making raw-milk cheese, which must be aged for a minimum of sixty days to destroy the bacteria in it, or pasteurized cheese, which requires heating the milk to destroy bacteria beforehand.

Milk pasteurization entered the marketplace in the early 1900s, when conditions for many cows and dairy operations were not ideal and were hard to regulate. Cows were not fed properly or cared for in ways that led to healthy milk production. The blanket solution was to pasteurize all milk products.

Unpasteurized milk, otherwise known as raw milk, is coming back into style, however, and many states are allowing small quantities to be sold from registered raw-milk sources and directly off the farm. Unpasteurized milk retains more flavor from the natural flora that the animals eat and has natural enzymes that aid digestion.

When it comes to Vermont cheese, the cheesemaking method will dictate whether raw or pasteurized milk is used. Most of the farmstead cheesemakers maintain small herds, who are fed grass during the summer and high-quality hay during the winter. The result is pristine milk that is high in vitamin A, vitamin B, and omega fats. This high-quality milk becomes cheese that is both delicious and healthy.

months will appear in the market in August. For those who love aged sheep's milk cheese, its best to stock up for winter enjoyment, for once the aged wheels are sold out, it will be another summer before more cheese will be available. Sheep's milk cheese is often lighter in color than goat's or cow's milk cheese and smooth in texture. Fresh sheep cheese has honey, citrus, and floral notes, while aged wheels, often referred to as tommes, develop rich caramel or butterscotch tones.

TYPES OF CHEESE

Fresh, Unripened Cheeses

Delicately flavored and creamy, the Vermont cheese in this category includes cream cheese, ricotta, mozzarella, mascarpone, quark, and fresh, creamy goat's milk cheese. The cheesemaking process involves milk that may or may not be cultured, but which in all cases has been pasteurized. The cheese has not been aged.

Fresh, Ripened Cheeses

Fresh, ripened cheeses also require pasteurized milk if they are sold before sixty days old. Many of the distinctive goat's milk cheeses known as chèvres or crottins fall into this category. These cheeses usually receive no particular rind treatment, except sometimes being sprinkled with *herbes de Provence* or layered with vegetable ash for color, and are left in a temperature-controlled environment for less than a week. The result is a lightly aromatic, subtly flavored cheese with a creamy texture.

Soft, Mold-Ripened Cheeses

These cheeses have had a specific mold culture added to the milk or misted onto the finished cheese to produce a soft rind that will ripen the cheese from the outside in. Often the healthy microflora is enhanced with moisture and a temperature-controlled environment, and these cheeses are carefully turned to allow even ripening. Brie and Camembert cheese styles, with their familiar bloomy rinds, fall into this category. These cheeses are usually made from pasteurized milk, if will be sold young, or raw milk if aged 60 days.

Semisoft Cheeses

To determine if a cheese is semisoft cheese, look for a firm yet springy consistency to its interior, combined with a natural rind—one that has been dipped in a salty brine, cider, or vinegar to give it an enhanced color and to give the ripening cheese a rich, fruity flavor. This category will also include Gouda and Monterey Jack, which more often than not are encased in wax rather than left to ripen in the air; yet both are mild cheeses, soft and pliable. Since semisoft cheese is typically aged for a minimum of sixty days, it can be a raw-milk cheese. Some semisoft cheeses will be softer when young, but can become a firmer cheese when aged for a longer period.

Hard Cheeses

The term *hard* applies to a cheese that has been aged for more than sixty days and that has a firm interior and concentrated flavor. Typically, Vermont aged cheddar falls into this category. After the cheese has been pressed to remove more than half the moisture, cheesemakers can choose to wrap the cheese in plastic or cloth, dip it in wax, or leave the natural rind (see below) before placing it in a temperature-controlled environment to age undisturbed and allow the cheese flavors to develop naturally.

Washed- or Brushed-Rind Cheeses

Many Vermont cheesemakers are producing a naturally washed-rind cheese, which is a cheese that is immersed in a salty brine, then lightly wiped with brine, beer, or balsamic vinegar several times a week until a healthy mold is established; the mold will assist the cheese in developing its true flavor. This process is called affinage and is carefully controlled and designed to encourage the growth of specific molds (especially those called *Brevibacterium linens*) and microflora in the cave environment. The process ultimately increases the breakdown of the interior of the cheese, which creates a complex flavor. Since the rind is all natural and part of the cheese, it's safe to eat, and often the layer just under the washed rind is packed with flavor. This washed-rind process can used for younger aged raw cheese ripened a minimum of sixty days, but it is more effective when the cheese is ripened for a minimum of three months—or, even better, five to six months or longer.

Blue Cheeses

A colorful addition to the cheese board, blue cheese offers a distinct bite that is achieved by a harmless mold in the cheese's interior, added during the cheesemaking process. The milk is inoculated with a specific mold culture, such as *Pennicillium roqueforti*. The curds are treated gently to preserve moisture and a loosely knit texture in the pressed cheese; air pockets remain that encourage an aerobic mold to bloom. Piercing the cheese with needles creates pathways to allow the blue veining to penetrate to the interior. Since this cheese is aged for sixty days, the milk can be either left raw (heated slightly) or pasteurized.

Blended/Flavored Cheeses

A blended cheese is typically a mild cheese that has a flavor mixed into the curd. Cumin, fennel, chili peppers, garlic, and dried nettles are some of the commonly added seasonings.

Smoked cheese is a flavored cheese that is pressed, cut into thin slabs and placed in a smoker that is smoldering with hardwood chips. The smoke infuses the exterior of the cheese, creating an essence that adds a distinctive finish and tawny coloring to the cheese.

Discovering

THE VERMONT
CHEESE TRAIL

County • by • County

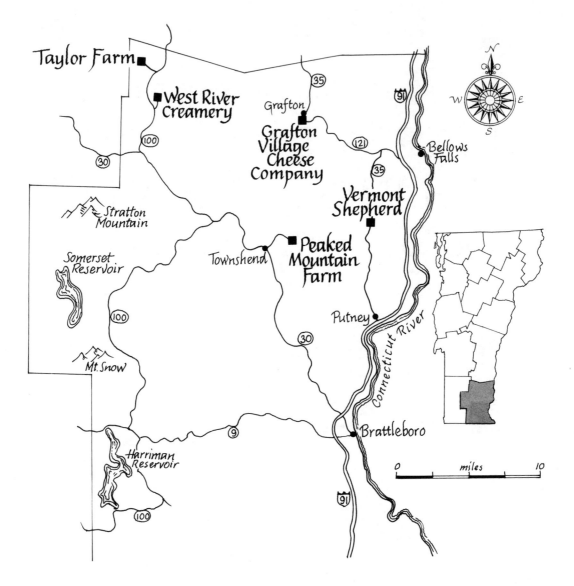

Taylor Farm

West River Creamery

Grafton

Grafton Village Cheese Company

Vermont Shepherd

Stratton Mountain

Somerset Reservoir

Townshend

Peaked Mountain Farm

Bellows Falls

Mt. Snow

Putney

Connecticut River

Harriman Reservoir

Brattleboro

35

91

121

35

100

30

100

30

9

100

91

N
W   E
S

miles
0   10

CHAPTER 1

WINDHAM AND BENNINGTON COUNTIES

Putney • Grafton • Townshend • South Londonderry • Londonderry

WINDHAM AND BENNINGTON COUNTIES ARE IN the heart of the Green Mountain National Forest, a popular tourist destination known for excellent hiking and skiing. Geographically, southern Vermont forms a narrow rectangle that starts at the southern tip of Lake Champlain and threads east across the Green Mountains to White River Junction. Composed of several distinct mountainous regions that run north to south—and that require the traveler to wind up and down over the terrain—each region has a unique soil, composition and landscape. The lush southern Vermont region has a variety of lakes and streams with majestic mountains and green valleys tucked in between, yet the region lacks the wide open vistas that characterize land hospitable for crops. Sheep and other livestock graze in the mountain conditions with great success, and the cheesemakers of this region make the most of their small flocks, and the rocky, yet fertile soil enhances the alpine flavor of their cheese.

The Connecticut River Valley forms a natural border with New Hampshire along the eastern section of the state, and farmers in the Windham and Bennington counties are blessed with rich soil. This area is also rich in agricultural history, which is evident in the old farmsteads that continue to thrive through several generations. Many of the venerable farms continue to operate in one form or another, producing milk and raising corn, grain, or vegetables. As these farms attest, perseverance, product diversity, and local supply and demand can sustain a small valley.

Award-winning **Vermont Shepherd** (1) is located on the Patch Farm, just north of Putney. The farm stretches uphill on land ideally suited for grazing sheep. The cheesemaking and caves are off limits to visitors, yet it's worth a drive to Patch Farm just to see the sheep grazing in the pastoral setting and to buy cheese at the self-serve farmstand.

Continue north, loop through Saxtons River and follow Route 121 into the classic Vermont village of Grafton, where a town green surrounded by clusters of white clapboard houses signifies community. **Grafton Village Cheese Company** (2) produces a fine artisanal cheese, but unlike the other cheesemakers in this chapter, they purchase milk from nearby farmers, thereby contributing to the local farm economy.

From Grafton, head south on Route 35 toward the town of Townshend. Before arriving at the town green, turn left up the 1.3-mile-long, steep dirt road to **Peaked Mountain Farm** (3). This former horse farm has remained much the same over the past several decades, although the farmhouse has been renovated and a modern cheesemaking facility has been built into the basement of the barn. Visitors are always welcome and cheese tasting is encouraged. The terrain here is rocky, and the sheep are spread out over several pastures, but a self-guided tour of the farmstead is an excellent way to experience a diversified small farm.

The next stop is Londonderry and the **West River Creamery** (4) on Middletown Road. This cheesemaker leases his facility from the landowner and purchases fresh milk from the dairy farmer at the Middletown Road Farm. Cheesemaking takes place several times a week, but it's best to call ahead to see if the day you want to visit is a cheesemaking day; if it is, you can watch the process from a picture window.

Continue north on Middletown Road to Route 11/30, turn left, and continue beyond Londonderry center, veering right on Route 11. Travel one mile to **Taylor Farm** (5). It's well worth stopping to taste cheese at the farmstand and to savor the romance of cheesemaking at the farm, with the cows grazing nearby or being milked in the barn. Visitors can peek around and see the essence of life on the farm. Taylor Farm has a long history of dairy, and farmer/cheesemaker Jonathan Wright is dedicated to saving this family farm. It is the pride of the community and one of the few remaining working farms in the region.

1. VERMONT SHEPHERD

DAVID MAJOR
875 Patch Road
Putney, VT 05346
(802) 387-4473
www.vermontshepherd.com

TYPE OF CHEESE: SHEEP'S MILK

➤ **Vermont Shepherd Tomme:** These semihard cheeses are aged in their own hand-built cave, on ash wooden boards that help in the development of natural rinds. Each day, trained staff turns, brushes, or washes the cheeses to cultivate the unique tawny exterior and allow the flavor to develop its characteristic nutty, caramelized notes.

ABOUT THE CHEESE

In 1993, Vermont Shepherd introduced its first cheese at the annual American Cheese Society (ACS) competition. It was an odd looking cheese—about nine pounds and completely dented and black with mold. But it was so astonishingly tasty, the company took home its first blue ribbon for farmstead cheese and just missed winning best of show.

Since then, it has consistently won awards for a semihard, natural-rind sheep cheese, which boasts a sweet, full flavor that reflects the farm's terroir, including the gentle flora of a healthy pasture. Milking just over 200 ewes—only during the summer months, when the sheep are pasture fed—the company finishes cheese production in November. Vermont Shepherd ages 20,000 pounds of cheese in its custom-built cave. Even at twenty dollars per pound, demand exceeds supply, and the cheese is usually sold out by the end of the winter.

WHAT MAKES THIS CHEESE SPECIAL?

From spring to fall, cheesemaker and shepherd David Major moves the milking ewes every twelve hours to a fresh grazing field, to make the most of the sweet herbs, grass, and wildflowers that grow rampant in the pasture and flavor the seasonal cheese. He treats the milk gently, warms it slowly, and follows a consistent cheesemaking method and recipe every time. Ash-wood shelves hold the wheels of cheese in the carefully controlled aging cave; this wood allows the cool, moist air to penetrate the cheese surface from all sides, and the mold that ripens the cheese develops naturally from spores inside the cave. A full-time *affineur*—a person who specializes in aging cheese—washes the natural rind twice a week. From the day the cheese is placed in the cave, it takes four months to ripen.

HOW TO VISIT

A self-serve farmstand stocks wedges of cheese year-round, seven days a week. A chalkboard at the stand describes events at the farm and where the ewes are currently grazing, encouraging visitors to get out of their cars to experience the farm. The cave, located farther down the winding driveway, is not open to the general public, but you can call ahead to arrange a visit. Cheese is also available via mail order from the company's Web site.

DIRECTIONS

From the center of Putney, take Westminster West Road approximately five miles to Patch Road. Turn right onto Patch Road and travel one mile to the self-serve farmstand, on the right.

ABOUT THE FARM

LIKE MANY YOUNG FARMERS IN 1970S, David and Cindy Major of Patch Farm were dedicated to preserving a way of life with a fierce commitment to the family farm. But cultivating new lambs for meat and wool was a hardscrabble existence and not profitable enough to keep the farm alive. The solution lay in finding a new way to use the sheep. Almost two decades after the Majors first started milking their herd and producing Vermont Shepherd cheese, the 200-plus-acre fields and 600-head flock flourish;

Visitors to Patch Farm, home of Vermont Shepherd cheese, can buy a tomme at the farm's self-serve farmstand.

however, Cindy is no longer part of the cheesemaking operation.

Many of the farm's Dorset-Freisan-Tunis-cross sheep are sold to other farms, leaving about 200 to milk for the company's award-winning cheese. The sheep are rotated into different fields to allow the wild thyme, mint, and wild geraniums to replenish. Several large, fluffy, white Maremma sheepdogs and a border collie hang close to protect the flock from coyote and other predators.

The cheese is made with only fresh milk, gathered every day. The milk is never frozen and never pumped, capturing the essence of the land in the flavors of the cheese. The sheep are milked in a milking room—located in the lower barn next to the main farm house—and the milk is transferred into twenty-six milk cans and transported to the cheese room in a barn near the upper fields.

Built in 1995, after the Majors made a trip to France to investigate how European cheese developed rich flavor, the legendary aging cave is designed to encourage the growth of taste-enhancing mold. The Majors learned that instead of fighting mold, as they had been taught, the French cheesemakers encourages a living rind. After tasting cheese aged in dark railway tunnels, old castles, and abandoned barn foundations, they determined that mold was the secret ingredient that their cheese had been missing, and they returned to Vermont determined to give their cheeses the French touch. It only took two months to dig their very own cave—complete with an Old-World stone façade decorated by trailing nasturtiums—into the hillside. The result is that Vermont Shepherd cheese has both a distinctive look and lush flavor unmatched by other local cheeses, and the family farm is now thriving, once again.

2. GRAFTON VILLAGE CHEESE COMPANY

533 Townshend Road

Grafton, VT 05146

(800) 472-3866

www.graftonvillagecheese.com

TYPE OF CHEESE: COW'S MILK

➤ **Premium Cheddar:** This raw-Jersey-milk cheddar is aged for one year and develops a characteristically sharp cheddar flavor and a creamy finish.

➤ **Classic Reserve:** Aged for two years and sealed in black wax, this signature product has won thirteen international awards. Milder than the extra-aged cheese, the raw-Jersey-milk cheddar product has a creaminess that offsets the sharpness.

➤ **Four Star:** Aged for over four years, this mature cheddar is dry and crumbly and has an exceptional creamy, long-lasting finish.

➤ **Five Star:** Aged for over five years, this dry-textured cheese is sweet and complex, with robust flavor and a smooth finish that provide a true melt-in-your-mouth sensation.

➤ **Stone House:** Aged for six years, this assertive cheddar has a dry, crumbly texture and a strong, complex, lingering flavor.

➤ **Maple Smoked:** Infused in cool smoke from a smoldering hardwood maple fire for four to six hours, this cheese is reminiscent of bacon and has unlimited breakfast potential.

ABOUT THE CHEESE

Cheddar is characteristically defined by terms such as "sharp" or "extra sharp," but Grafton prefers to classify its cheese by the number of years it has aged—a system that more accurately reflects the cheese's flavor components. The buttery color is due to the Jersey milk, which has exceptionally high butterfat and high protein. The milk is delivered daily from the Agri-Mark Dairy Co-op, which collects it from farms within a 150-mile radius. The cheese is naturally aged in a state-of-the-art, cool-air facility that maintains an even 45 degrees—a temperature that allows the cheese to ripen slowly.

WHAT MAKES THIS CHEESE SPECIAL?

Grafton likes to claim that the term *cheddar* is a verb meaning "doing something," which describes the classic method for making cheddar cheese. For over forty years, cheesemaker Scott Fletcher has been "teaching milk to be cheese" in a slow process that involves cutting the curds into slabs, then flipping and stacking them to slowly release whey. They are then milled into smaller pieces, salted, and pressed

into molds. The result is dry cheddar with a smooth, creamy consistency and finish. Selecting milk from only Jersey cows is the key to the smooth, creamy mouth feel, which tempers the sharper bite characteristic of most cheddar.

HOW TO VISIT

Visitors are welcome to visit the company's store from Monday through Friday, 8 A.M. to 4 P.M., and on Saturday and Sunday from 10 A.M. to 4 P.M. Cheesemaking takes place six days a week, during two shifts a day, and can be viewed from picture windows at the visitors' center. Tasting samples are available, and cheese is for sale from the store's cooler.

DIRECTIONS

Although Grafton is off the beaten path, several roads lead to it. It is best to check a map to find the best route. From Interstate 91, take exit 5 at Bellows Falls and drive Route 121 through Saxtons River and Cambridgeport to Grafton. Turn left at the Grafton Inn and follow Route 35 about half a mile to the cheese factory on the left. Ample parking is available, and there are grounds for strolling and picnics.

Grafton Village Cheese Company, in the heart of picturesque Grafton Village, has a visitors' center, where guests can view the cheese-making operation.

ABOUT THE COMPANY

GRAFTON VILLAGE CHEESE COMPANY produces 1.5 million pounds of award-winning, aged cheddar cheese each year from its facility in the heart of picturesque Grafton Village. That amount will increase in the near future with an expanded facility located in Brattleboro. The humble beginnings of Grafton Village Cheese Company go back to 1892, when Grafton Cooperative Cheese was founded to turn milk from the local farms into cheese and thus give the farmers a way to preserve their excess milk. In 1912, the cheese factory burned, and no cheese was produced until 1965, when Dean Mathey established the Windham Foundation. A graduate of Princeton and the retired chairman of the Bank of New York, Mathey discovered Grafton when he summered there as a young boy with his family. Concerned that this rural community had no industry to support its basic infrastructure, Mathey established the foundation (named after Windham County) to restore and revitalize Grafton Village. A nonprofit organization, the Windham Foundation began restoration of half of the town's buildings. Four years later, with the help of the University of Vermont, it rebuilt the cheesemaking facility, replacing the wood vats with modern steel. They asked local farmer and cheesemaker Edward McWilliams to reestablish the factory, which was built on his dairy farm. The same year, Scott Fletcher, having just graduated from high school, applied for the job as a cheesemaker. Forty

Grafton Village Cheese Company produces 1.5 million pounds of cheddar each year at its facility.

years later, he is the head cheesemaker, turning the slabs of cheddar by hand and strewing handfuls of salt over them to release they whey—a salting method he calls "feeding the chickens."

Fletcher has never taken a cheesemaking class or traveled to England, where the original Cheddar is made. Yet he instinctively knows what to do with the raw Jersey milk, heating it to 155 degrees for ten seconds, then cooling it to 88 degrees. In the early years, animal rennet started the fermentation, but that practice was discontinued in 1987, as animal rennet had become expensive and hard to find. Vegetarian-approved rennet is now used. Once the cheese has been pressed, it is vacuum sealed, labeled by lot and year, and stacked on shelves in the warehouse to age.

The sweet buttery aroma from cheesemaking wafts up to the second floor of the cheese-making facility, where vice president Peter Mohn moved into the corner office in 1991. Taking a leading role with the Vermont Cheese Council, he attends trade shows all over the country and was one of the first to recognize that American palates were ready to move beyond sharp cheddar to the more robust flavor that the aged cheddars provide. After putting aside the young cheese that would typically sell in the first two years, Grafton began to introduce three-, four-, five-, and six-year-old cheddars. The company is currently developing a natural-rind, animal-rennet, cave-aged traditional cheddar that will be available in limited quantities.

3. PEAKED MOUNTAIN FARM

ANN AND BOB WORKS
1541 Peaked Mountain Road
Townshend, VT 05353
(802) 365-4502

TYPE OF CHEESE: SHEEP'S MILK, COW'S MILK

➤ **Vermont Dandy:** This natural-rind, semihard, aged cheese is made from raw sheep's milk; it has complex floral flavors, grassy overtones, and a light aroma of toasted pecans.

➤ **Ewe-Jersey:** This natural-rind, aged cheese—50 percent sheep's milk, 50 percent cow's milk—is sweet and nutty, rich and smooth, with hints of the various herbs found in the fields.

ABOUT THE CHEESE
Peaked Mountain Farm produces about 6,000 pounds of aged cheese over five months, including a Romano-like cheese and soft-style cheeses similar to Camembert and Brie. All are made on the premises from raw sheep's milk or a combination of sheep and cow milk. Peaked Mountain pure sheep's milk cheese is dense, well aged, and has a natural rind and a fruity kick.

WHAT MAKES THIS CHEESE SPECIAL?
Ann and Bob Works were part of the first wave of Vermont cheesemakers to apprentice with David and Cindy Major at Patch Farm, and their cheese is very similar to Vermont Shepherd's in quality and consistency. Bob and Ann make their cheese in small batches, using raw milk from their own herd. They work together to make sure that their herd is well tended and frequently moved to different fields, so the animals always have optimal pasture to graze on. The cheesemaking facility is next door to the milking parlor.

HOW TO VISIT
Visitors are welcome to visit the farmstand, which is open seven days a week, year-

round, and to see the onsite cheesemaking from May to October. You can also watch the eighty sheep graze in the surrounding fields or take pictures of the friendly miniature Sicilian donkeys that protect the sheep from predators.

DIRECTIONS

Just past the town green in Townshend, across from the Grace Cottage Hospital, take a right turn onto Peaked Mountain Road. The yellow sign indicates the farm is 1.7 miles up, yet the rocky road makes it seem farther. The farm straddles both sides of the road. Park in front of the barn.

ABOUT THE FARM

SEVERAL MILES UP A NARROW DIRT ROAD, the type that requires pulling over to the side if another car is approaching, Peaked Mountain Farm, with its 100 acres, 1800s farmhouse, and big red barn, perches over the town of Townshend like

Peaked Mountain Farm owners Ann and Bob Works stand behind their Vermont Dandy and Ewe-Jersey cheeses.

an ancient sentinel. Bob and Ann who retired early from corporate jobs to pursue the farming life, purchased the former Morgan horse farm in the 1990s and converted it into Peaked Mountain Farm, LLC. The historic house was renovated with an open floor plan, a spacious kitchen for entertaining, and a new wing to accommodate a gracious mudroom. The exterior remains much the same as it was for centuries, but the old barn across the dirt road from the house is now a year-round farmstand and cheesemaking facility. The sheep live nearby in an open-sided barn.

Bob and Ann describe Peaked Mountain as a "food farm." Their primary occupation is producing a unique series of farmstead cheeses using milk from their own sheep. The farm also has an artisanal bakery and a slaughterhouse where lamb and pork are processed for restaurants and farmstand customers. A sugar-house produces over 100 gallons of maple syrup each year, and the whey from the cheesemaking is put to good use fertilizing 250 blueberry bushes. The Works sell their bread, meat, and cheese at the Brattleboro Farmers Market and host farmhouse dinners in their spacious kitchen several times during the year to introduce customers to their way of life and give them a taste of farm-fresh cuisine.

Ann is the primary cheesemaker, while Bob handles the livestock and crop rotations and markets the cheese. They breed East Friesian sheep for their high milk production and gentle demeanor, and the flock numbers close to a hundred. Lambing season starts in April, and the new lambs are allowed to stay with their mothers for a month before being weaned and sold for meat. Eighty ewes

Wheels of Peaked Mountain cheese rest on plastic shelves and begin to develop a natural bloomy rind from the microflora present in the aging room.

remain for milking. Cheese production begins in May and runs for the next five months. A state-of-the-art cheesemaking facility and two temperature-controlled aging rooms help make this historic farm a thriving modern business.

4. WEST RIVER CREAMERY

JANE AND CHARLIE PARANT

P.O. Box 536

Middletown Road

Londonderry, VT 05148

(802) 824-6900

TYPE OF CHEESE: COW'S MILK

➤ **Middletown Tomme:** A brushed-rind cheese with a smooth, creamy interior.

➤ **Cambridge:** This English-style cheddar is moist like a Colby, yet ages quickly and achieves a full, complex flavor at five months. It is available in applewood-smoked and hickory-smoked varieties.

➤ **Londonderry:** An English style, farmhouse, Cheshire type, this cheese has a dry texture and a peachy color. The young cheese has a milky, salty flavor that mellows with age.

➤ **Farmhouse Jack:** Mild, smooth, and milky sweet, this cheese is ideal for melting and cooking.

➤ **Three Mountain:** This soft, washed-rind cheese is slightly salty, velvety smooth, and has a bold flavor.

ABOUT THE CHEESE

West River Creamery is a moderate sized operation, producing about 1,600 pounds of cheese a month or approximately 19,000 pounds per year. Several types of cheeses are crafted here, from natural rinds to traditional English-style cheddars, and aging times vary from seventy days to eighteen months, depending on the type of cheese. The cheese is naturally aged in a humidity-controlled environment and then packaged in plastic.

WHAT MAKES THIS CHEESE SPECIAL?

Charlie Parant learned the art of cheesemaking twenty years ago when he and Jane raised goats and made cheese in their home kitchen. After a decade as a biology teacher, he turned into a professional cheesemaker, working at Boggy Meadow in Walpole, New Hampshire. The cheesemaking business is separate than the dairy operation at Middletown Farms, the home of West River Creamery, and this allows Charlie to concentrate on cheesemaking, rather than care of the farm and the animals. Milk is piped directly from the milking parlor into the cheese vats, and the cheese is made in small batches only one day a week. To achieve a creamy texture, the curds remain still after they are cut, instead of being constantly stirred, as is done in a typical cheddaring process. Keeping the curds still allows them to absorb more liquid, which results in a smoother final product.

HOW TO VISIT
Call ahead to find out when cheesemaking takes place, since it is only once or twice a week. Visitors are welcome to watch from the small room overlooking the cheese room and can purchase cheese at the farm or local farmers' markets.

DIRECTIONS
Traveling on Route 100, at the bridge in South Londonderry, take Middletown Road, which travels uphill. Pass the Village Pantry du Logis on your right and travel one mile to the farm, which will be located on the left side of the road.

ABOUT THE COMPANY

MIDDLETOWN FARMS, named after the road that connects the village of Londonderry to South Londonderry, is one of the most scenic farms in southern Vermont and has 200 acres of healthy fields that straddle the road. Downhill from the main barn, the cheese room is tucked neatly into the same building as the milking parlor, and a Georgian-style, yellow farmhouse is situated across the driveway.

In 1977, there were sixteen working dairy farms within a thirteen-mile radius of Middletown Farms, yet today there are only three. Much of the land has been secured in a Vermont Land Trust, thanks to former senator Ed Janeway and his wife, who moved there in

Slabs of Middletown Tomme are weighed and packaged at West River Creamery.

1945 and raised six children. Dairy farming has always been more about a way of life and less about profit, and dairy farming on this farm is no exception. Conservation and preservation were foremost in the minds of Barry and Wendy Rowland when they became land stewards and purchased the farm in March of 1997. While it hasn't always been profitable, it has remained a continuously operating dairy farm, and the size of its herd and the nature of the business have evolved over the past half century.

Recognizing the importance of maintaining the land and the operations, the Rowlands encouraged the dairy farmer at the time to start making cheese with the milk from his 100-head herd of Holstein and Jersey cows. They hired consultant and cheesemaker Peter Dixon to help develop suitable recipes, design the cheese room, and install the equipment. Cheesemaking began at the farm in 2000, and the product was dubbed Middletown Farm Cheese. After two years, the farmer decided to move to a new location, taking his cows and leaving the cheese room empty.

Luckily, his daughter, Amy, and her husband, Nick Stone, decided to take over the farming operation. The Rowlands purchased a herd of sixty-nine Holstein and Jersey cows from a neighboring farm that was going out of business. Yet the cheese room remained empty for two years, until Charlie Parant heard about the vacancy and contacted the Rowlands, who welcomed him to their farm. The cheesemaking and the dairy are kept as separate entities, yet they work together to create a quality farmstead cheese and a working farm that makes the community proud.

5. TAYLOR FARM

JONATHAN AND KATE WRIGHT

825 Route 11

Londonderry, VT 05148

(802) 824-5690

www.taylorfarmvermont.com

TYPE OF CHEESE: COW'S MILK

➤ **Vermont Farmstead Gouda:** Sealed in red wax, this is a traditional, unadulterated, raw-milk Gouda. Semisoft and aged a minimum of two months, this washed-curd cheese's mild flavor has buttery qualities. It is also available lightly flavored with chipotle peppers, garlic, cumin, caraway, or nettles.

➤ **Vermont Aged Gouda:** The gem of the farm's Goudas, wheels of this cheese are made with the same recipe as the Vermont Farmstead Gouda, then aged at least one year. The result is a firm, intensely flavored cheese that is more complex than traditional Gouda. The farm produces a very limited supply.

➤ **Maple Smoked Gouda:** This cheese is made the same way as the traditional Gouda made famous by the Dutch, but the rounds are smoked at nearby Grafton Village Cheese Company with maple wood smoke and sealed in brown wax. Milder than hickory-smoked cheeses, this consistently popular cheese continually wins awards.

ABOUT THE CHEESE

Taylor Farm Gouda's fresh, pure, buttery flavor has won numerous ACS awards. Traditionally made from Holstein milk and requiring two months of aging, this cheese is made with a warm blend of Holstein and Jersey milk that is sent directly from the milking parlor to the cheese vats.

WHAT MAKES THIS CHEESE SPECIAL?

Taylor Farm's Vermont Farmstead Gouda is a raw-milk, washed-curd cheese, which means that during the cheesemaking process, half the whey is drained and replaced with hot water. The water cooks the curd and dilutes the whey so the acidity level doesn't rise as fast, making Gouda a little sweeter and smoother in texture than cheddar. Once the curds are pressed and the cheese formed, it is waxed and placed on wood shelves in a windowless, temperature-controlled room for sixty days or longer. The farm's aged Gouda is more intensely flavored than other American Goudas and more typical of the European style of the cheese.

HOW TO VISIT
Cheesemakers Tamry Underwood and Karen Carleton are in the cheese room making Gouda every Monday, Wednesday, and Friday. Visitors are welcome to visit the year-round cheesemaking facility, though it is best to call ahead for times. Cheese is available for sale or sample-tasting at the farm seven days a week. A visit is an ideal way for all ages to experience of life on a true working farm. Combine your visit with sleigh rides in the winter.

DIRECTIONS
Take Route 11 West from Londonderry Center, and the farm is one mile on the right. Drive past the farmhouse to the driveway that leads to the red barn.

ABOUT THE FARM

THE PASTORAL VIEWS of Taylor Farm's 560 acres spread across Route 11, the main thoroughfare heading west over the mountain to Manchester or east towards Bellows Falls. Draft horses graze in fields near the road, cows mingle in the barnyard, and a large red tractor mows hay in the summer and hauls the bales and manure across the busy highway during the winter.

Taylor Farm has been a working farm since the 1920s, when the Taylor family purchased the land and leased it to a series of tenant dairy farmers. Jonathan Wright worked at the farm as a teenager during the summer, when the Ameden family was in residence. In 1989, he and

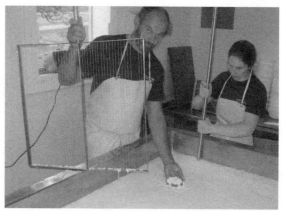

Farmer/cheesemaker Jon Wright tests the temperature of the milk before cutting the curds to separate the whey.

A young Jersey cow—future milk producer at Taylor Farm.

his wife moved into the farmhouse and started milking a herd of forty-four Holsteins and a few Jersey cows. For years, they sold milk to the Agri-Mark cooperative, but the fixed milk prices were too low to allow them to maintain the farm. In September 1998, the Wrights took one day's worth of milk and, instead of selling it to the milk co-op, made it into cheese. The rest is, as they say, history.

The Wrights recently purchased the farmhouse and part of the land from the Taylor family, leaving the surrounding hills and fields in a land trust, so those pastoral views can remain forever. While they continue to sell milk to Agri-Mark, and the herd has grown to close to 100 head, cheese production has become their main focus, and they package close to 70,000 pounds of choice Gouda per year. Jon is currently the president of the Vermont Cheese Council, and their year round farms and offers a choice selection of Vermont cheese from other local farms.

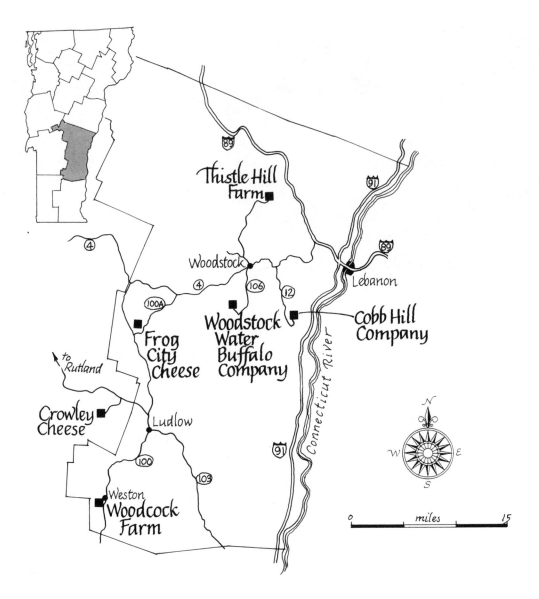

Thistle Hill Farm

Woodstock

Cobb Hill Company

Lebanon

Frog City Cheese

Woodstock Water Buffalo Company

to Rutland

Crowley Cheese

Ludlow

Connecticut River

Weston
Woodcock Farm

N
W E
S
miles

0   miles   15

36

CHAPTER 2

WINDSOR COUNTY

Weston • Healdville • Plymouth Notch • South Woodstock
North Pomfret • Hartland Four Corners

INDSOR COUNTY SHARES THE BORDER OF NEW Hampshire along the Connecticut River, running from the southern city of Springfield north to Norwich, and forms the eastern part of southern Vermont. This region is rich in history; the birthplace of President Calvin Coolidge and home of Plymouth Cheese Company are located within twenty miles of the Crowley Cheese factory, the first cheesemaking facility in Vermont. The county's hills and valleys are full of quintessential Vermont farmhouses and barns, along with state parks and small lakes. This county has long been a thriving farm community, and working farms continue to make the best of the rich, fertile soil along the Connecticut River. Today, many of the farms are small; their houses and barns have been lovingly renovated and are home to a wide variety of cheesemakers.

From Londonderry, head north on Route 100 towards Weston and watch for a sign on the right. The flock of sheep grazing near the road is a sure sign that you have arrived at **Woodcock Farm** (1), where a winding driveway ends at an open-sided barn and cheese room. Cheesemaking takes place every day at this farm and can be viewed through a glass window. Be sure to ask for samples and check the cooler for cheese to buy, before continuing north to Ludlow. From there, turn left onto Route 103 to the small town of Healdville, where the **Crowley Cheese** (2) factory sits on the back side of Okemo Mountain, one of southern Vermont's largest ski areas. Healdville is an unlikely place to find a cheesemaker, yet Crowley is a National Historic Landmark and the oldest continuously operated cheese producer in the United States. The Crowley Cheese factory is a three-story building built in 1882. It was originally one of the fifty-eight cheese cooperatives that existed in Vermont and is well worth a visit to watch the cheesemaking, which takes place four days a week.

Back onto Route 103, travel east and turn to go north on Route 100 until it meets Route 100A at Plymouth Union. Head towards Woodstock on Route 100A but take a left into Plymouth Notch to experience the small village store and tour the historic houses. **Frog City Cheese** (3) is located at the former Plymouth Cheese Company, which was established by John Coolidge, the president's son who engaged cheesemakers in the area during the mid-1900s. The newly updated facility is open during the summer; visitors can watch the cheesemakers at work through plate-glass windows and nosh on cheese samples in the same historic building that served as a cheesemaking cooperative a hundred years earlier. Stroll upstairs to view antique cheese molds and other implements, along with photographs that depict the cheesemaking process.

Continue north on Route 100A until it meets Route 4, which goes to Woodstock. From Route 4, go south on Route 106 to South Woodstock, passing through upscale horse country, and watch for a sign on the right to **Woodstock Water Buffalo Company** (4). Replacing Holsteins with water buffaloes may be an odd choice, yet these quiet animals rest peacefully in the pastures and in the barn, and the growing business of water buffalo mozzarella and yogurt provides a ready market for their milk. Visitors are welcome to watch the cheesemaking, although not much is done by hand.

The road from Woodstock to North Pomfret is one of the prettiest in the state, with well-tended farms and barns around every corner. Just before reaching **Thistle Hill Farm** (5), be on the lookout for a picturesque orchard that sweeps along the landscape in perfect rows, a reminder that the farmers who lived in this valley had a diverse range of agricultural capabilities. The farmhouse and barn at Thistle Hill rest on a small plateau with a backdrop of steep pastures. The owners chose to raise Jerseys not only for the high butterfat in their milk, but also for the cows' strong legs and capacity to graze and climb hills.

Cobb Hill (6) is located to the south, in Hartland Four Corners, a small rural town just east of Hartland, with easy access to nearby Interstate 91 and Ascutney Mountain and Resort. Preserving this former working dairy farm as a cheesemaking facility and vegetable garden for the cohousing members and neighbors is paramount among the goals of the Cobb Hill community. Through careful thought and planning, Cobb Hill has restored the farming way of life and in the process created an active educational experience for others.

1. WOODCOCK FARM

MARK AND GARI FISCHER

P.O. Box 21

Weston, VT 05161

(802) 824-6135

TYPE OF CHEESE: SHEEP'S MILK

➤ **Weston Wheel:** Made from raw milk and aged a minimum of four to six months, this natural-rind tomme has an exceptionally sweet, nutty, toffeelike essence.

➤ **Summer Snow:** Soft ripened, with a bloomy rind, this raw-milk cheese is cool and creamy, like a Camembert, and has hints of mushroom and lemony butter. It is available only during peak summer months.

➤ **West River Feta:** Tangy with a creamy smooth texture, this raw-milk feta is also available marinated in olive oil and herbs—a favorite with local customers.

ABOUT THE CHEESE

Woodcock Farm currently makes three distinct types of cheese with several variations throughout the year, during the short five-month season that their ewes are grass fed and produce milk. Summer Snow is a true delicacy and has a gentle white mold that ripens the cheese from the outside in. Weston Wheel, named after the farm's location, is a Pyrenees-style tomme. It has a smooth, honey-colored natural rind, classic sheep's milk cheese characteristics, and a complex flavor that develops over the palate and leaves a clean finish.

WHAT MAKES THIS CHEESE SPECIAL?

This small family farm is focused on producing a high-quality product while maintaining a year-round flock of sheep; this multifaceted business means balancing spring lambing and crop rotation with milking and cheesemaking. So far, the Fischers manage to do it all, including making cheese in a postage-stamp-size cheese room. The milk that the sheep produce during their early summer grazing yields the richest tasting cheese, and Woodcock Farm follows a production schedule that allows Mark and Gari to make cheese from this early summer milk. Mark and Gari are both cheesemakers and keep careful notes to match their recipes with the seasons and the milk.

HOW TO VISIT
Cheesemaking takes place regularly from late May to September. Visitors are welcome, and can watch the cheesemaking through a viewing window. Cheese is for sale at the farm upon request or at summer farmers' markets and specialty stores throughout New England.

DIRECTIONS
Woodcock Farm is located on Route 100 between Weston and Londonderry. Look for the sign on the road that indicates the gravel driveway, which winds down past the red colonial house and ends at the farm.

ABOUT THE FARM

DURING THE 1940S, dairy farmers Anna and Casper Woodcock owned the old Woodcock Farm, which straddles Route 100 between Londonderry and the historic village of Weston. But in 1981, they sold the herd of forty Holsteins and the 200 acres of agricultural land to a real estate agent, who put 50 acres into conservation and turned 100 acres into home sites. The remaining 50 acres were deemed a useless floodplain, but only due to lack of vision. In the mid-1980s, Mark and Gari Fischer bought the land, reclaiming it as a pasture for their sheep, and the once scrappy acreage had a new lease on life.

Wheels of freshly made Summer Snow rest on open shelves in the cheese room at Woodcock Farm.

During the spring lambing season, an open-sided barn at Wood-cock Farm is crowded with ewes and almost twice as many lambs.

The Fischers first pursued cheesemaking as a part-time business, but now it is a full-time obsession. Their colonial-style farmhouse overlooks forty-five acres of lush organic pastures on the rich floodplain of the West River, where their flock of East Friesian sheep, a breed highly regarded by cheesemakers, grazes. The sheep's healthy diet gives the farm an ample supply of milk for the several types of rich, buttery-flavored cheese.

During the spring lambing season, an open-sided barn is crowded with ewes and almost twice as many young offspring. A border collie, Maremma sheepdog, llama, and three ponies shelter nearby, then protect the herd from coyotes once it returns to the open pasture at the onset of summer. Newborn lambs nurse for one month before they are sold. The milk is gathered in the milking room and piped directly into the cheese room. This routine continues for the next five or six months, until the end of lactation, when the flock will return to the fields. In the winter, the sheep come back to the open-sided barn to keep each other warm, allowing the vibrant pasture to sweeten for next summer's grazing. Currently limited by the short milking season, the size of their flock, and a small space for cheesemaking and affinage, the Fischers hope to expand their facility. In the meantime, they produce exceptional, one-of-a-kind farmstead cheese that reflects their skills as shepherds and talented cheesemakers. Several times during the year, they share their knowledge and host cheesemaking classes held at their farm and spacious home kitchen.

2. CROWLEY CHEESE

14 Crowley Lane
Healdville, VT 05758
(802) 259-2340 or (800) 683-2606
www.crowleycheese.com

TYPE OF CHEESE: COW'S MILK

➤ **Colby:** Aged from two months to one year, this raw-milk Colby has all the best qualities of a mild New England cheddar. Following a classic cheddar recipe, the curds are rinsed with water before pressing, which gives the resulting cheese a sweet, moist finish. Wrapped in cloth and aged in wax, the cheese is available as a full wheel or logs. The same Colby recipe is also blended with garlic, dill, sage, and other classic herbs to heighten the flavor profile.

ABOUT THE CHEESE

Each week, 5,000 pounds of milk per day are delivered to the Crowley Cheese factory, and four days a week, 500 pounds of cheese is made each day with much the same recipe and methods as the original Crowley Cheese was made in 1882. Only a few changes have been made to update the recipe, and the wooden cheese molds have been replaced with stainless steel. The current cheesemaker, Ken Hart, learned his craft from the previous cheesemaker, who was trained in traditional methods. This sweet, mild Colby is similar to a cheddar; the mild version is aged a minimum of two to four months, and the extra sharp is aged nine to twelve months.

WHAT MAKES THIS CHEESE SPECIAL?

The recipe and the cheesemaking process is essentially the same as that for cheddar cheese; however, the curds are rinsed with spring water to release the acids and heighten the moisture. Instead of being slabbed, the curds are tossed by hand; it takes six pairs of hands to turn the curds and drain the whey before it knits together. Once the curds are salted, a fine mist is sprayed over the top to reduce the acidity and create moisture that will add to the unique character of the cheese. The cheese molds are filled and pressed, then the cheese is removed from the molds and dipped in wax before it is transferred to the temperature-controlled rooms for natural aging.

HOW TO VISIT

Visitors will see a time-honored process of making cheese. The whole process starts early in the morning and takes six and a half hours, so try to time your visit sometime between late morning to early afternoon for the most action. Visitors can view the process through a picture window, and a screen door to the cheese room allows conversations to flow between visitors and cheesemakers. Crowley general manager Cindy Dawley is often either making cheese or answering questions about the company. Cheesemaking takes place from Tuesday through Friday, from January to October.

DIRECTIONS

From Ludlow, take Route 100 north to Route 103 west to Healdville. The factory store, where cheese and other products are available, is on the left. Continue for another mile, turn left onto Healdville Road, and travel two miles to the factory.

From Rutland, take Route 103 to Mount Holly and continue towards Healdville. Turn right onto Healdville Road and travel two miles to the factory.

The factory is on the left side of the road; park next to the building.

ABOUT THE COMPANY

THE CROWLEY FAMILY BEGAN MAKING CHEESE in 1824 in the kitchen of their farmhouse, located behind what is now the Crowley Cheese factory. Winfield Crowley and his wife, Nellie, built the factory in 1882, after demand for their cheese outpaced supply. Using milk from their own herd and daily deliveries from neighboring farmers, the Crowley family began a business that continues in much the same way as it has for over 150 years. The factory was the first cheese factory in the state and possibly the nation. The thriving business quickly became the hub of activity for the area. Crowley cheese became so popular that neighbors were recruited to age the cheese in their cellars in return for all they could eat. Many participated, and the arrangement proved to be an excellent way to deal with the storage crunch.

The demand for Crowley artisanal cheese has always been strong, and while much of the cheese was sold in stores throughout Vermont, wheels were also shipped to Boston and New York. Winfield and Nellie's son George continued the business, then passed it to his son Robert and his brother Alfred, who operated the local post office out of the farmhouse. It was an agreeable arrangement for the cheese business; Robert would make the cheese, while Alfred would pack and ship it.

In 1964, Alfred sold the original homestead and the family's 100 acres to Randolph Smith, a summer resident who lived next door. Smith was retiring from his job as headmaster of the Little Red School House in New York City, and because of his interest in Crowley cheese, he maintained the historic elements of the farm and the business. The cheesemaking facility has been updated only slightly since its inception—a more modern cheese press was added and the vat was replaced in the 1960s, yet cheese is still made in the original cauldron. When Cindy Dawley, the general manager of the factory for the past twenty-one years, tells visitors about the history of the company, she describes how everyone who came into the cheese room to buy cheese used to help stir

Cheesemakers at the Crowley Cheese factory fill antique cheese molds with washed curds for the company's Colby.

the milk and cut the curds. (New state regulations later put an end to the practice.)

Crowley Cheese continues to be a well-run
operation and is owned cooperatively by twenty-
one shareholders. The factory produces approximately 88,000 pounds of cheese each year, most
of which is sold via mail order. In fact, mail
orders are the major source of revenue for the
business, and the factory is closed between
November and December to ship holiday orders.

*Cindy Dawley has been the general manager of the
Crowley Cheese factory for more than twenty years.*

3. FROG CITY CHEESE

TOM GILBERT AND JACKIE McCUIN
106 Messer Hill Road
Plymouth Notch, VT 05056
(802) 672-3650
www.frogcitycheese.com

TYPE OF CHEESE: COW'S MILK

➤ **Plymouth Cheese:** Available in young, mature, and select varieties, this granular-curd, or stirred-curd, cheese is made from raw milk. It is tangy, rich, open bodied, old fashioned, and uncomplicated. The same recipe is available in smoked, crushed red pepper, rosemary, caraway, cider-soaked, garlic, and sage flavors.

ABOUT THE CHEESE

Plymouth Cheese is characterized as a granular-curd cheese, which is moister than cheddar, yet has many of the same flavor attributes. Moderately sweet, buttery, and low acid, it develops a tangy quality as it ages. The curds are constantly stirred to prevent the whey from knitting prior to going into the molds—a method that produces a creamier texture than traditional cheddar. Fresh curds were once sold from the factory, but due to Vermont pasteurization laws, these are no longer available.

WHAT MAKES THIS CHEESE SPECIAL?

Plymouth Cheese is an heirloom, and the recipe would have been lost, if not for those who preserved the factory and remembered the original cheesemaking process and the way the cheese should taste. Plymouth Cheese has a distinct creamy quality that is due to the way the curds are cut, stirred, and pressed. Once a week, 12,000 pounds of fresh Vermont milk is delivered from local farms and pumped into a refrigerated storage tank. Three days a week, the cheese is made according to an exact recipe developed by careful observations and historic accounts. The cheese is wrapped in gauze and transferred into a cooler to dry for about week. Then it comes out to be wrapped in cellophane and waxed before entering the aging room for a minimum of sixty days.

boundary that kept visitors from entering the room. But now visitors must watch the process from behind a large plate-glass window.

HOW TO VISIT

Open year-round, the Frog City Cheese factory and retail shop are open daily, 9:30 A.M. to 5 P.M., late May to the end of October. An exhibit on the factory's second floor uses period graphics and the original 1890 factory equipment to explain the story of cheesemaking in Vermont.

When John Coolidge was making cheese, a rope strung between the retail store and the cheese vats was the only

DIRECTIONS

From Ludlow, turn north onto Route 100. Follow Route 100 until it meets Route 100A at Plymouth Union. Take Route 100A towards Woodstock and watch for signs into Plymouth Notch. Turn left into the Coolidge historic site, then turn left at the village store. Frog City Cheese is on the right, and parking is to the left of the factory.

ABOUT THE COMPANY

PLYMOUTH NOTCH HAS ALL THE QUALITIES of a picture-perfect historic small town preserved in time. White post rails lead to a small compound of white buildings, with a post office and general store at the center. President Calvin Coolidge was born in the building next to the general store on July 4, 1872, and moved to a larger house across the street, where he summered with his family.

The Calvin Coolidge State Historic Site in Plymouth Notch is considered one of the best-preserved presidential sites in the nation. In addition to the homestead, church, barns,

Tom Gilbert and Jackie McCuin produce huge, tasty wheels of Plymouth Cheese at the Frog City Cheese factory in Plymouth.

and dance hall, visitors may tour the Plymouth Cheese factory, which is currently the home of Frog City Cheese. Built by Colonel John Coolidge (the president's father), James S. Brown, and three other local farmers in 1890, the factory has produced a legendary granular-curd cheese for over a century.

In 1895, there were fifty-eight cheese factories in Vermont, and each served as a convenient outlet for the fresh milk produced on area farms. The Plymouth Cheese factory closed in 1934, but was reopened by the president's son, John, in 1960. The Vermont Division for

49

Wheels of clothbound and waxed Frog City cheese rest on open steel shelves in temperature-controlled rooms, just as they did when the Coolidge family made cheese at the factory.

Historic Preservation purchased the factory from John Coolidge in 1998, on the condition that they find someone to continue making the cheese.

For the next several years the division worked closely with other state agencies and the Vermont Cheese Council members to bring the building up to state-mandated code, while preserving its historic character. Most of the equipment in the cheese room remains from when John Coolidge was making cheese in the 1960s, including the giant milk vat, which holds 5,000 pounds (600 gallons) at a time; the drain table; the metal cheese molds; and the sideways press that extracts the final dregs of the whey. The two-story aging rooms, located in the same building, are also the same as they were in the 1960s.

On October 1, 2004, Jackie McCuin and Tom Gilbert leased the building from the state and established Frog City Cheese, named after a small settlement nearby. Tom and Jackie upgraded the factory with new equipment and made improvements to the building. Ready to start, they had everything except for the recipe for how to make the legendary Plymouth Cheese. Nothing was written down. With the assistance of Jean Hoskison, who made cheese for John Coolidge, they pieced together the steps in the cheesemaking process and tasted every batch to evaluate how closely it resembled the original recipe. Finally, they were able to re-establish production of the historic Plymouth Cheese granular-curd cheese.

4. Woodstock Water Buffalo Company

P.O. Box 295

South Woodstock, VT 05071

(802) 457-4540

www.woodstockwaterbuffalo.com

TYPE OF CHEESE: WATER BUFFALO'S MILK

➤ **Water Buffalo Mozzarella:** A fresh, firm, coarse texture and buffalo-milk whey incorporated into the "spaces" in the body of the cheese make this farmstead cheese close to the true Italian Mozzarella.

ABOUT THE CHEESE

Woodstock Water Buffalo Company is currently the only Vermont cheesemaker producing fresh mozzarella with water-buffalo milk. Water-buffalo milk is considered the best milk for producing mozzarella cheese, because of its 9- to 10-percent butterfat content (compared to cow's milk's 3 to 4 percent) and 4.7 percent protein content. The company's original animals were brought to Vermont from Florida, Arkansas, and Texas, and an Italian cheesemaker was hired to produce an authentic cheese.

Woodstock Water Buffalo Mozzarella is made fresh once a week, from pasteurized milk collected at the farm.

WHAT MAKES THIS CHEESE SPECIAL?

Keeping the herd and an open barn close to the cheesemaking facility allows the company to create a truly fresh product. The milk is piped directly from the dairy into the cheese room; culture is added, and the whey is drained and fed back to the animals. While the cheesemaking process is largely industrial, a trained cheesemaker watches it closely, because there is a ten-minute window for the cheesemaker to capture the cheese at the exact moment that it reaches perfect elasticity.

HOW TO VISIT

Visitors are welcome to Woodstock Water Buffalo Company, although there are no formal tours available. Cheese production takes place one to two days a week. The cheese room is open to the public and separated from the factory by a plate-glass window. Visitors can watch the cheesemaking process, though it mostly takes place in large stainless steel vats, and take pictures with the water buffalo. Visitors can also watch the company's popular water-buffalo yogurt being made.

DIRECTIONS
From the town of Woodstock, take Route 106 south to South Woodstock. At the Kedron Valley Inn, turn right onto Church Hill Road and go half a mile. Turn left onto the dirt driveway, passing a field with grazing water buffalo, and follow the driveway up to the top of the hill. Park near the barn.

ABOUT THE FARM

EVERYTHING LEADING UP TO the Woodstock Water Buffalo Company (formerly known as Star Hill Dairy) is quintessential Vermont, starting with the picturesque village of Woodstock, which is full of stylish shops and galleries. Just outside town, it's horse country, with riding rings and classic barns. Slightly further on, the Vermont scenery takes an unusual twist. Although there are grand houses surrounded by verdant pastures, instead of cows, horses, or sheep, two dozen Asian water buffalo quietly graze in the fields. These large, docile black animals with horns that curl around to their chins belong to the only water-buffalo-milk creamery in the United States.

The farm's milking herd consists of 220 animals, part of a herd of 500 to 550 or so that are located on two different farms. Most are kept in the open-sided barn and let out to graze for a few hours during the day; all contain a computerized tag in their ears that sends information about their food, milk, and general whereabouts back to the farm's command center, located in the high-tech dairy barn.

The water buffalo quietly standing in the open-sided barn seem to have adjusted to the cacophony of hissing sounds generated by the cooler fans and air-conditioning units buzzing. The farm is an industrial setting, a modern dairy facility that includes a stall-free barn complex, which allows the animals to roam, and a tandem milking parlor. The animals are fed all-natural hay and grain and are grazed during their dry period—the sixty to ninety days prior to calving.

In order to keep up with demand for its products, the Woodstock Water Buffalo Company encourages dairy farmers interested in switching from milking cows to explore the benefits of water buffalo. So far, only a few have made the switch. While it is unlikely that water buffalo will replace the traditional Vermont cows and sheep, yogurt and cheese produced by these unusual animals is more than just a novelty.

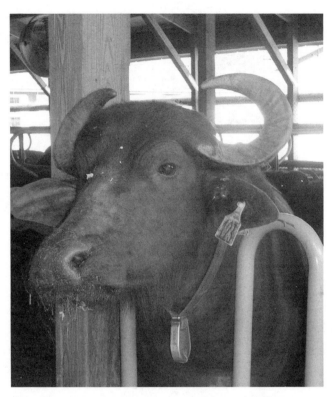

One of the stars of the show at Woodstock Water Buffalo Company, the only Vermont cheesemaker producing fresh mozzarella with water-buffalo milk

5. THISTLE HILL FARM

JOHN AND JANINE PUTNAM

P.O. Box 255

107 Clifford Road

North Pomfret, VT 05053

(802) 457-9349

www.thistlehillfarm.com

TYPE OF CHEESE: COW'S MILK

➤ **Tarentaise:** This aged, raw-milk, organic farmstead cheese is smooth textured. It has subtle notes of toasted nut and hints of caramel, and its complex finish fills the mouth with flavor. The distinctively curved natural rind is formed in the traditional alpine cheese molds.

ABOUT THE CHEESE

Thistle Hill Farm's Tarantaise is handmade from the certified-organic milk of grass-fed Jersey cows. The cheese's warm butterscotch color is evidence of the milk's high beta-carotene content and intensifies close to the natural rind, so it is best to cut the cheese into full slices rather than cubes. The distinctive flavor is characteristic of Alpine cheese sought out by the Putnams during their extensive travel and research in the French and Swiss Alps.

WHAT MAKES THIS CHEESE SPECIAL?

The high cream, fat, and protein contents of Jersey milk enhance the flavor of this Swiss-style cheese. The copper cheesemaking vat at Thistle Hill Farm was custom built in Switzerland and imported in March 2002; the copper is essential to proper flavor development in the aged Tarantaise cheese. Cultures, which give the cheese its distinctive flavor profile, are imported from France, and the Putnams make their own rennet using whey from the previous cheesemaking. Rennet making adds an extra, carefully controlled step to the cheese-making process and is one of the keys to the Putnams' richly flavored Tarantaise.

The curds are transferred by hand from

the vat into cheesecloth, then pressed into molds imported from France. The molds are then turned up to five times to create the cheese's distinctive concave sides, which are similar to those of Beaufort and Abondance, two fine cheeses from the Savoy region.

The aging room is made mostly of stone. During the aging process, which takes a minimum of five months, the cheeses are turned and scrubbed at least twice each week so that they develop a natural rind and warm butterscotch color. John makes his cheese intuitively and understands that cheese is sensitive to all types of environmental conditions, including weather and any changes in the plants the cows have been eating.

HOW TO VISIT
"Nobody is invited, but everybody is welcome," says John, and since this is a small family farm, it's best to call ahead for visits by special arrangements. Cheese is for sale at the farm, and cheesemaking can be viewed through a window.

DIRECTIONS
From Woodstock, take Route 12 north to Pomfret Road. Bear right toward Suicide Six and South Pomfret. Travel about four miles to South Pomfret, then take the right fork around the general store to North Pomfret. Pass a white church and take a left turn onto Caper Road, across from the red post office. Travel 0.6 mile, turn left onto Clifford Road, and up the first driveway on the left.

ABOUT THE FARM

THE PRISTINE VIEW FROM THE FARMHOUSE on Thistle Hill Farm, where John and Janine Putnam live with their four children, three dogs, and assorted livestock, is of graceful sloping meadows. Just over two dozen Jersey cows graze in these meadows, steadily moving uphill as the grass turns green. A family vegetable garden runs along the driveway across from the house, and a small barn provides shelter to

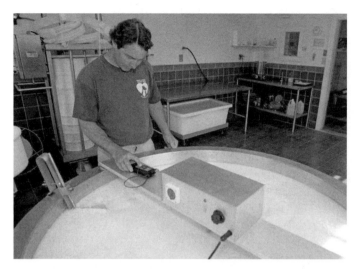

Thistle Hill owner and cheesemaker John Putnam checks the temperature of the milk in the copper vat before adding rennet for Tarantaise cheese.

the cows, plus a few pigs during the summer. It is a picture of purity: simple and clean.

The Putnam's bought the eighty-three-acre farm in 1986 and rebuilt the dairy barn and outbuildings. They grazed beef cattle the first ten years to bring the pastures back to a healthy meadow. Dedicated to organic agriculture from the start, they switched over to raising dairy cows and sold milk to Organic Cow, a milk cooperative.

In 2000, after spending a summer traveling around Italy, France, and Switzerland in search of a cheese that they both loved, they found one in Beaufort, a small village in the Savoy region of the French Alps. They also found that distinctive blend of soil, geography, climate, and flora that gives cheese from the Tarantaise region of France its characteristic smoothness, subtle nut flavor, and complex finish are similar to the conditions found in Pomfret, Vermont. After speaking to numerous cheesemakers, they returned home with a plan to reproduce an alpine cheese on their own farm. It took two years before they had everything in place, including a new cheesemaking facility with natural-pine-paneled walls, a large cheesemaking and affinage room, and a sprawling office with an adjoining family room and guest quarters. They invited a cheesemaker from France to the farm to give technical assistance and made their first cheese on July 5, 2002.

Janine and John conduct their farm responsibilities like a well-choreographed dance; Janine mostly tends to the breeding and feeding of the herd, while John does the milking and

Janine Putnam hangs out a large section of cheesecloth to dry in the yard after a cheesemaking session. Photo courtesy of Thistle Hill Farm.

develops the cheese. Cheese is made from April to December, since the Putnams refuse to make cheese when their cows are eating winter silage. From their herd, they breed and "tie 20," or milk twenty cows, for the entire milking season. The milk doesn't make enough aged cheese to meet demand, but the Putnams are more committed to quality than quantity. From harvesting their own organic hay to creating a unique, organic Vermont cheese, everything the Putnams do reflects their personal commitment to quality.

6. COBB HILL

5 Linden Road
Hartland/Four Corners, VT 05049
(802) 436-4360
www.cobbhill.org/cheese

TYPE OF CHEESE: COW'S MILK

➤ **Ascutney Mountain:** This cheese has a natural rind the color of summer straw and a sweet, nutty flavor similar to Comte or Appenzeller and other alpine cheeses. Its firm texture comes from the buttery-rich Jersey milk and sometimes small crystals, called grana, are evident in the aged cheese, as are naturally formed small holes (eyes).

➤ **Four Corners Caerphilly:** Developed from a Welsh Caerphilly recipe, this natural-rind cheese is cheddared and salted in a vat, pressed, and aged for a minimum of two months. Similar to the Ascutney Mountain, yet designed to be ready as a younger cheese, the product has flavor profile that is toasty and caramelized.

ABOUT THE CHEESE

Cobb Hill began its year-round cheese production in December, 2000, and currently has a working partnership with six members' of the Cobb Hill community who are cheesemakers: Judith Bush, Phil Bush, Gail Holmes, Marie Kirn, Sophie Starr, and Zach Stremlau. The raw, whole milk used in this cheese comes exclusively from the farm's small herd of grass-fed Jersey cows. The animals are raised on pasture maintained and improved without chemical fertilizers. In winter, organic grain and hay raised to organic standards on the farm are fed to the cows. Vegetable rennet is used in making both cheeses.

WHAT MAKES THIS CHEESE SPECIAL?

Cobb Hill cheesemakers are highly aware

of the changing seasons and the effect they have on their cows' milk—effects that are often evident in the color of the cheese once it has aged. The early spring pasture makes the cows' milk rich in butterfat, and the resulting summer cheese turns a deep golden yellow; the fall-winter cheese, produced as the fields start to turn brown, develops a sharper flavor, full of earthy overtones, and is paler in comparison. Made in small batches from a herd of well-tended cows, the cheese is named after the nearby mountains that looms over the valley and Four Corners, where the farm is located.

HOW TO VISIT

Visitors are welcome to purchase cheese from a self-serve refrigerator in the farm's gambrel barn, but the cheesemaking room is small and cannot routinely accommodate observers. Visitors are asked to call ahead with requests to see the facility or glimpse the cheesemaking process. On

Saturdays from May through October, Cobb Hill cheese is marketed directly to consumers at the Norwich, Vermont, farmers' market.

DIRECTIONS

From Woodstock, follow Route 4 east to Route 12, and take Route 12 south to Hartland Four Corners. At the Four Corners crossroad, turn left onto Mace Hill Road. Cobb Hill is the first left, Linden Road. The farm buildings are immediately visible after turning.

Cobb Hill cheesemaker Zach Stremlau fills cheesecloth-lined cheese molds before setting them under the custom-made wooden press to further drain the whey from the curds.

ABOUT THE FARM

ALL THE PARTNERS involved in Cobb Hill cheese are members of the Cobb Hill Cohousing Community, an experiment in sustainable development and community living. The cheesemaking business is part of the residential community, which includes a cluster of newly built, energy-efficient homes and a shared common house, all perched on a hill overlooking the old farm. In 2006, forty adults and twenty-one children were living at the Cobb Hill community.

A resident Jersey cow basks in the sun at the farm of the Cobb Hill cohousing community.

There are three components to the Cobb Hill community: a research and training institute, a working farm, and a residential neighborhood. The research and training component is a nonprofit organization called the Sustainability Institute, which has offices located in the renovated farmhouse. Farm-related businesses or enterprises at Cobb Hill are managed either by the community as a whole or by subsets of community members who have invested in and work in them. These businesses include a five-acre vegetable- and flower-garden enterprise, dairy cows, sheep, meat birds and egg-laying hens, honeybees, maple-syrup production, cheese production, and stewardship of 30 acres of pasture and 230 acres of woodland. Cobb Hill residents make efforts to reduce their footprints on the environment, improve the community's 260 acres of land, and create a positive social environment for its multiage residents. The cheese enterprise provides a guaranteed market for the excellent milk of the community herd, thereby supporting the livelihood of the farmers and the members' commitment to creating a sustainable food system.

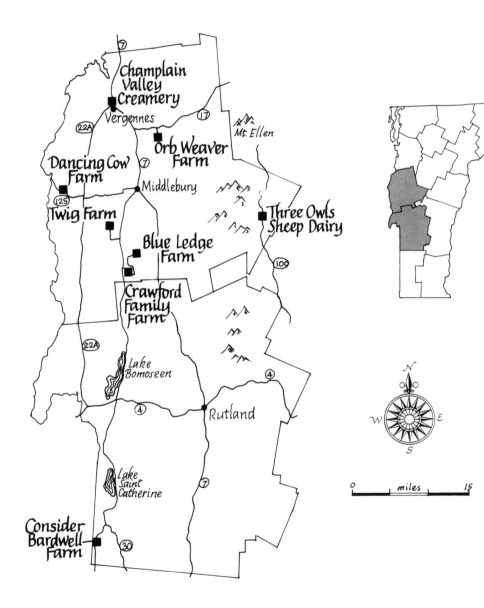

Champlain
Valley
Creamery

Vergennes

Mt. Ellen

Orb Weaver
Farm

Dancing Cow
Farm

Middlebury

Twig Farm

Three Owls
Sheep Dairy

Blue Ledge
Farm

Crawford
Family
Farm

Lake
Bomoseen

Rutland

Lake
Saint
Catherine

Consider
Bardwell
Farm

N

W   E

S

0   miles   15

62

CHAPTER 3

RUTLAND AND ADDISON COUNTIES

*West Pawlet • Salisbury • Whiting • West Cornwall • Bridport
Vergennes • New Haven • Granville*

HE FARMS IN RUTLAND AND ADDISON COUNTIES, with their rich soil seeping in from the proximity to Lake Champlain and flat, expansive fields surrounded by mountains in the distance, are undisputedly located in the best agricultural valleys in the state. It is breathtakingly beautiful farm county, and this land has been popular with dairy farmers for generations. Many dairy farms remain dedicated to Holstein cows and the convenience of the dairy co-op trucks that pick up milk. There is a change afoot, however, as cheesemakers breathe new life onto the farms in these counties, and it is no surprise that the highest concentration of Vermont cheesemakers is located in this region.

Start with a drive through one of the most scenic and prosperous farm valleys in the state, the Mettowee Valley, to West Pawlet for a stop at **Consider Bardwell Farm** (1) in the southernmost region of the county. The brick farmhouse, long white dairy barn, and brick outbuildings was once a summer home to Consider Bardwell, who established a butter and cheese factory here back in the early 1900s. The farm's chamois-coated Oberhasli goats romp in the fields, and visitors are welcome to watch them, as well as view cheesemaking through a glass picture window and purchase cheese from the refrigerator at the farm.

Follow Route 30 north past Lake St. Catherine and Lake Bomoseen to Whiting, a small farming community in the heart of dairy country. Turn right at Leicester and head north towards Salisbury to visit **Blue Ledge Farm** (2), which consists of a small blue farmhouse with white trim, an empty silo, and remnants of the concrete foundation once used for silage—all evidence of a former dairy farm. This small farm has been revived with a flock of goats that are fed only the best hay and happily prance in the fields and blue ledge outcroppings that surround the farm.

Down the road, neighboring **Crawford Family Farm** (3) farm raises Ayrshire cows. This unusual brown and white variety is known for their strong jaws and sturdy frame and is best suited to grazing in pasture rather than staying inside the barn. Ayrshire milk contains extra fat globules that are particularly beneficial for cheesemaking, and Vermont Ayr cheese is breathing new life to this second-generation family farm.

Twig Farm (4), in West Cornwall, is proof that farming and cheesemaking don't require an old farm, barn, and lots of equipment. In the basement of the sleek, architect-designed home, the owners age their award-winning cheese to perfection. The cheese itself is made next door in an artful cheesemaking facility connected to the garage.

From Cornwall, turn left onto Route 74 and the right onto Route 22 to Bridport to find **Dancing Cow Farm** (5). The traditional Vermont farmhouse and red barn are built atop of a knoll featuring a 360-degree view of the valley. From there the owners can easily watch their cows, who come into the barn only to be milked.

Follow Route 22 to Vergennes and **Champlain Valley Creamery** (6), located on the second floor of the Kennedy Brothers Factory Marketplace. The building was originally constructed for use as a creamery in the early 1900s and has now come full circle, albeit on a much smaller scale. Watch as the thick cream from local organic dairies is hand-turned into delectable cream cheese.

Travel south on Route 7 to New Haven, turning left before the center of town onto Lime Kiln Road. You are entering pure Vermont farm county, featuring fields of corn alternating with fields of grazing cows, all set in a rural neighborhood of modest farmhouses and barns. **Orb Weaver Farm** (7) closely manages a small herd of Jersey cows, just enough to keep the fields healthy and provide enough fresh milk for its prize-winning farmhouse cheese. Balancing a summer market garden with winter cheesemaking, this two-woman family farm continues to provide an inspiring model for others cheesemakers. Finally, Dan Hewitt of **Three Owls Sheep Dairy** (8), on the easternmost edge of the Green Mountains, makes cheesemaking look easy at his small facility.

1. CONSIDER BARDWELL FARM

ANGELA MILLER AND RUSSELL GLOVER

1333 Route 153

West Pawlet, VT 05775

(802) 645-9928

www.considerbardwellfarm.com

TYPE OF CHEESE: GOAT'S MILK, COW'S MILK

➤ **Mettowee:** The farm's signature cheese, this fresh, creamy, pasteurized, goat's milk chèvre is light and lemony with distinct flavors of the summer pasture.

➤ **Danby:** This firm yet crumbly, salty, raw-milk cheese in the Greek feta style is made from goat's milk and aged in brined whey.

➤ **Manchester:** This aged, washed-rind, raw-goat's-milk peasant tomme has a nutty and earthy rustic nature. The flavor changes based on the rotational grazing of goats on the pastures and the aging process itself.

➤ **Experience:** The fresh Mettowee is cave aged to produce this sharp, tangy cheese with a gorgonzola-like flavor.

➤ **Dorset:** This aged, raw-milk, washed-rind Jersey milk tomme is made during the mid-season from milk from a neighboring dairy farm. The flavor and texture varies, yet typically reflect a distinctive blend that is reminiscent of a Danish Havarti and Italian Alpine cheese.

ABOUT THE CHEESE

Cheesemaking began at Consider Bardwell Farm in 2003 with a fresh goat's milk cheese, dubbed Mettowee for the river that flows through the farm's valley. Since adding a temperature-controlled aging room to the barn, Consider Bardwell Farm offers an aged, semisoft goat's milk cheese and fragrant, aged tommes, made by combining raw goat's milk with cow's milk. Made in small batches from the farm's own goat's milk and neighboring farm's cow's milk, all of the cheese has a consistent quality, and new varieties continue to evolve.

WHAT MAKES THIS CHEESE SPECIAL?
The goats, the milking parlor, the cheese-making facility, and the cheese affinage rooms are all under one roof in the converted cow barn. Consider Bardwell Farm is best known for its soft Mettowee, but the fragile nature and limited shelf life of this cheese has led the farm to experiment with an aged crottin and fill in the season with cheeses that incorporate local cow's milk. Thanks in part to a nearby bee-keeper, the healthy meadows are resplendent with a range of wildflowers, and the essence of those flowers is reflected in the floral nature of the cheese.

HOW TO VISIT
Visitors are welcome year-round to watch the goats romp in the surrounding fields, and cheese is for sale in a self-serve cooler. The cheese is also available in local country stores, at farmers' markets, and in specialty food shops in New York City.

DIRECTIONS
From Route 30 in Pawlet, travel north two miles and turn left onto Route 153 to West Pawlet. The center of town is a small cluster of mostly vacant buildings. Turn left at the roundabout and bear right past the fire station. Travel two miles, and Consider Bardwell Farm is on the right, indicated by the sign with a distinctive goat logo.

ABOUT THE FARM

*L*OCATED IN THE SOUTHERNMOST SECTION of Addison County, a few miles from the New York state border, the 300-acre Consider Bardwell Farm remains one of the most impressive farms in the valley. From 1864 to 1932, the farm collected fresh milk each day from surrounding farms to make cheese and shipped big wheels of cheddar on the Dayton-Hudson Railroad that ran through the property along the Indian River to Albany, Boston, and beyond. Consider Stebbins Bardwell (1785–1866), the

The Oberhasli goatherd at Consider Bardwell Farm includes approximately fifty milking goats.

farm's founder, was hugely successful at dairy farming, cheesemaking, slate quarrying, and tool making.

When Angela Miller and Russell Glover bought the three-chimney brick farmhouse in 2001, it came with the three brick outbuildings and a large dairy barn. Sitting at their kitchen counter, they weren't content just to admire the beautiful view. They decided to bring Consider Bardwell's legacy back to life, raising livestock and producing cheese on the old farm once again. But the livestock and the cheese would be different this time around.

Angela and Russell started with a small herd of goats, known as Oberhasli, recommended by a farm intern who had studied cheesemaking in France. Though the breed was not common in this country, a breeder was located in New Hampshire, and Angela drove over in her station wagon to pick up their first goats. She had never even seen a goat until there were six of them in the back of her car. But when she saw their perky ears, chamois coats, black noses and hoofs, and

The red brick farmhouse and white dairy barn at Consider Bardwell Farm date back to the 1900s, when the farm's eponymous owner established a butter and cheese factory there.

ridge of black running down their backs, it was love at first sight.

After the first year, the herd grew to a total of nineteen Oberhaslis and has more than doubled each spring since; it now totals approximately fifty milking goats. Many of the cheese names are derived from the local geography and from Consider Bardwells family names, thus connecting this farm back to its origins. Consider Bardwell may not have thought of goats, but he would be proud to know his memory lives on in the soft, smooth cheese produced on his old farm.

2. BLUE LEDGE FARM

GREGORY BERNHARDT AND HANNAH SESSIONS

2001 Old Jerusalem Road

Salisbury, VT 05769

(802) 247-0095

www.blueledgefarm.com

TYPE OF CHEESE: GOAT'S MILK

➤ **Lakes' Edge:** This soft-ripened cheese is marbled with blue ash, which creates a stunning layered effect and earthy flavors.

➤ **Crottina:** Covered in white mold and aged three to four weeks, this dainty cheese is based on a French crottin and has a decadent velvety texture.

➤ **La Luna:** This white-waxed, raw-milk cheese, aged three months or longer, is similar to a mild-tasting Gouda and has a firm and smooth texture.

➤ **Chèvre:** Available in plain, herbal, and pepper varieties and sold in four- to six-ounce rounds, this clean-tasting cheese has floral highlights.

➤ **Riley's Coat:** This raw-milk, washed-rind cheese is aged for over four months. It has a gentle taste and is good for slicing, melting, and grating.

ABOUT THE CHEESE

Gregory Bernhardt and Hannah Sessions have been making cheese since 2002. They currently produce five different types of goat cheese, each one unique in color, texture, and flavor. They milk their own herd of about seventy-five goats from April to November, after which they purchase milk from a neighboring farmer, who alternately breeds his goats so they let down their milk on an opposite schedule, thus guaranteeing fresh milk year-round. The cheese is made in small batches. Once it has aged the proper length of time, it is wrapped in breathable, clear paper, just before it is shipped to a loyal following of wholesale markets and stores or sold at farmers' markets.

WHAT MAKES THIS CHEESE SPECIAL?

Gregory takes an artist's approach to cheesemaking and credits his Italian heritage and love of cooking for his ability to create his own recipes. "It's the perfect blend of art and science," he explains. He often experiments with new cheese recipes to reflect the best of the season's milk, and Hannah takes extra care to be sure her animals are well grazed and healthy.

Each handmade cheese is carefully turned and monitored during the aging process. Lake's Edge is an exceptional cheese and reflects Gregory's experience and practice. Named after the rocks found on Lake Champlain, the creamy-smooth cheese is drained for two days, flipped, and dusted with a light layer of vegetable-based blue ash (otherwise known as *cendre*) that is imported from France; the ash is also pressed between two layers to appear in the center as well as the exterior. The cheese ages for forty-five days, and the result is a sweet, soft-ripened cheese with an earthy twinge.

HOW TO VISIT
Call ahead for visiting hours and tours, since the family is often busy with farm chores or cheesemaking. The farm's cheese is available at local co-ops and farmers' markets.

DIRECTIONS
Take Route 30 to Whiting Four Corners. Turn onto Leicester Road and travel three miles to Leicester Junction. Go over the bridge, cross a set of railroad tracks, and turn left onto Old Jerusalem Road. Follow Otter Creek for 2.2 miles. The farm is on the right.

ABOUT THE FARM

BLUE LEDGE FARM looks like a classic Vermont painting. The dirt road that runs alongside Otter Creek leads to a lupine-blue farmhouse with a white picket fence, the home of Gregory Bernhardt, Hannah Sessions, and Blue Ledge Farm cheese. A towering silo—leftover from the former dairy—rises alongside the driveway, along with a converted barn and milking room. The barnyard nestles between the

A sampler of Blue Ledge Farm's cheeses (clockwise from upper left): Lakes' Edge, Riley's Coat, and herb-covered chèvre

house and the cheese room, and getting to the cheese room requires dodging chickens, children's toys, a compost pile, and bales of fresh hay.

Gregory and Hannah moved to Blue Ledge Farm in 2000 after a short stint in Italy, which led them to a passion for cheese, and a six-month search for the right farm to raise goats and make farmstead cheese. When they found Blue Ledge Farm, named after the ribbon of blue slate that runs under the farmhouse and through the barnyard, indicating a rocky soil, they knew they had found the right place for goats.

On her parents' farm in nearby Cornwall, Hannah tended a small flock of sheep and then apprenticed on a dairy farm in Massachusetts. Her passion for dairy led her to take responsibility for raising and rotating the 100 goats on the 130 acres of pasture and bringing them into the barn for milking twice a day. Hannah and Greg purchased used cheese equipment and set up a modest, yet functional cheesemaking room with a temperature and humidity-controlled aging room. There, Greg makes close to a hundred pounds of cheese each day. The goats graze from April to November, eating scrub bush, bark, thistle, and stinging nettles to create sweet milk for the cheese.

In addition to raising two young children, goatherding, and cheesemaking, both Greg and Hannah are artistic painters. That artistry finds its way into their unique varieties of goat cheese, making Blue Ledge Farm an inspiration for cheese connoisseurs.

3. CRAWFORD FAMILY FARM

SHERRY CRAWFORD

165 Sawyer-Needham Road

Whiting, VT 05778

(802) 623-6600

www.crawfordfamilyfarm.com

TYPE OF CHEESE: COW'S MILK

➤ **Vermont Ayr Farmstead Cheese:** This natural-rind, semihard, aged, alpine-tomme-style cheese has a rich, full body, complex flavor, and fresh, lingering taste.

ABOUT THE CHEESE

The recipe for Crawford Family Farm's Vermont Ayr Farmstead Cheese is based on a northern Italian Fontina-type cheese. Aptly named after both the breed of cow whose milk is used and the Vermont fresh air that feeds the pastures. The firm, natural-rind cheese is soft and fragrant with a pale yellow color and creamy texture.

WHAT MAKES THIS CHEESE SPECIAL?

Minute butterfat globules make Ayrshire cow milk distinctive and result in a cheese that is smooth, creamy, and sweet. Cheese-

The roof of the oldest barn at Crawford Family Farm bears the name and date of the farm's original owner. The Crawford family has turned the grand floor of the barn into a cheesemaking facility and aging room.

making follows cheesemaker Maria Trumpler's old-fashioned technique and begins in a kettle-shaped vat within an hour of milking. Relatively new to the Vermont cheese scene, Crawford Family Farm has concentrated on a single product, which it makes in small batches with a minimum of culture so the pure flavor of the milk shines through in true farmstead-cheese style.

HOW TO VISIT

The 1910 barn houses the farm's cheese-making facility, as well as young heifers. Cheesemaking is done four times a week and can be viewed through a picture window into the cheese room. Call ahead to arrange visits and tours.

DIRECTIONS

From the center of Whiting, turn onto Leicester Road and then take a right onto Sawyer-Needham Road. Travel for one mile to the white house with a gray barn on left.

ABOUT THE FARM

THE HERD OF DEEP RED-AND-WHITE COWS grazes in fertile fields along Sawyer-Needham Road in Whiting. Ayrshires, a hardy breed originating in Scotland, are known as excellent grazers and are the most stylish of the dairy cattle. They are also on the American Livestock Breeds Conservancy's watch list because the number of registered Ayrshires has declined significantly in recent years. However, since the 1950s, the Crawford family's Scapeland Farm has been breeding and milking registered Ayrshires on its lush 330 acres.

Siblings Sherry, Cindy, and Jim Crawford inherited the farm from their parents. In an attempt to diversify and maintain the family farm, they partnered with cheesemaker Maria

Trumpler to create a recipe that highlights the unique quality of the Ayrshire breed's milk. Vermont Ayr was launched in the fall of 2005 and has already developed a healthy following.

The slate roof of the oldest barn is inscribed with the name and date of the original farm owner: "A. C. Needham, 1910." The family gutted the lower half of the barn that housed calf pens and turned it into a pristine cheesemaking facility and aging room for Vermont Ayr cheese.

Crawford Family Farm's border collie waits patiently in front of the barn.

In a typical farm-family style, all pitch in as needed: Jim tends to the milking, haying, and marketing; Cindy raises the calves, manages the breeding program, and does marketing; Sherry assists in all phases of the production and marketing of the cheese. Though she has a master's degree in biology and doctorate in the history of science, cheesemaker Maria Trumpler admits that she applies eighteenth-century cheesemaking methods to her work today; she uses the power of observation, writes everything down, and then steps back to allow the cheese to develop naturally in the cave, left to maintain its own natural level of humidity.

The Crawford family has many generations of experience with the Ayrshire breed, and this experience manifests in the delicacy and uniqueness of its farmstead cheese. Conserving and preserving the family farm, a heritage breed, and a historic barn are key to this cheese operation, and the Crawfords boast that some of their cows are direct descendants of the original Ayrshires from fifty years ago. Like other Vermont cheesemakers, they stay closely connected to the health of their herd, and in spring, summer, and fall they welcome Violet, Borenna, Selma, and all the others to graze upon lush pastures that surround their farm.

4. TWIG FARM

EMILY SUNDERMAN AND MICHAEL LEE

2575 South Bingham Street

West Cornwall, VT 05778

(802) 462-3363

www.twigfarm.com

TYPE OF CHEESE: GOAT'S MILK, COW'S MILK

➤ **Twig Farm Goat's Milk Tomme:** An intensely flavored, highly fragrant, semi-hard, natural-rind artisanal cheese is made with raw goat's milk. Aged for several months and carefully turned to create an exquisite composition.

➤ **Twig Farm Square Cheese:** This is an aged, raw goat's milk cheese. The texture of the cheese is semisoft, and the rind is natural and rustic in appearance. Uncooked and unpressed, the cheese is formed in a tied cloth that gives it a squarish shape. In the middle of the cheese is an indentation from where the knot was tied.

➤ **Twig Farm Soft Wheel:** This aged cheese is made with a mixture of raw goat's and cow's milk. The texture is semisoft and as the cheese ages, the rind is washed with whey brine, which creates a natural, smooth, turmeric-colored rind.

ABOUT THE CHEESE

Michael Lee trained as a cheesemonger for half a dozen years before launching his own venture, he learned to recognize the signs of truly delicious, highly specialized cheese. At Twig Farm, Lee is dedicated to producing cheese in the European tradition that reflects the quality of his land. The farm's animals graze in a young forest that has an abundant undergrowth of wild herbs, wildflowers, young trees, and shrubs, all of which contribute overtones to the cheese.

Cheese is traditionally named after the location where it is made, but Michael names his cheese simply by the way it looks: like a tomme, or a wheel, made with fresh goat's milk, cow's milk, or a combination. All of his cheeses are made from fresh milk poured into milk cans, chilled in a cooler, and transferred into the cheese room across the hall in the garage/barn.

The drained cheese is cured in brine and then aged on ash shelves in a moist cheese cave, located in the basement of the farmhouse. The cave's air temperature is maintained at a perfect 53 degrees. Michael turns each cheese at least forty times, patting it to spread the naturally created black molds evenly across the surface and thus create the cheeses' distinctive flavor.

WHAT MAKES THIS CHEESE SPECIAL?

All of Twig Farm's cheeses are made by hand and lovingly aged in their own cave. The first few wheels that emerged from the aging cave in the spring of 2006 were gray and knotty on the outside, but inside had creamy texture with light, high notes from the early spring milking. The mold-ripened cheese is sold as two-and-a-half-pound cylinders or five-pound wheels; the wheels can be cut into wedges to order, but are better if sold as a whole. The cheese can continue to ripen and its distinctive flavor

can continue to develop if it is left whole, rather than be cut and locked into plastic, which will retard the cheese's natural process. Michael and Emily manage the goats with strict attention to their diet and their pasture rotation. Michael also buys cow's milk from a nearby farm to use alone for winter cheese, or blend for a unique cheese flavor.

HOW TO VISIT

Call ahead to arrange for a farm visit and get directions.

DIRECTIONS

Provided by prior arrangement only

Rounds of Twig Farm's natural-rind cheese are immersed in a salty brine before being placed on the shelves for affinage.

ABOUT THE FARM

Unlike other young farmers, who buy old farms and renovate them to suit their needs, Emily and Michael Lee decided to create their own goat dairy farm from scratch. Calculating that it was cheaper to build new to their own specifications, they purchased twenty acres of land in West Cornwall from Emily's father in 2003.

Michael Lee, cheesemaker at Twig Farm, holds a raw-milk cheese he's dubbed "square cheese," which is formed in a tied cloth, rather than a cheese mold, to give it the unusual indentation.

With help from an architect and the dairy inspector's regulations, they designed a modern house and barn that incorporates their farm and cheesemaking business into a neat and tidy homestead.

They named their new place Twig Farm, after the young trees and scrub brush that had been cleared for the farm and house. But today, "Twig Farm" a misnomer, because the new, striking, grass-green house and barn blend seamlessly with the now-lush landscape.

The farm's three-dozen Alpine goats happily graze in the backyard on a rich diet of honeysuckle, plantain, cinquefoil, chicory, goldenrod, and nettles—all of which grew as the result of clearing the land. There is plenty for the animals to eat, and the richness of their diet is concentrated into the unique, full flavor of Twig Farm cheese.

Twig Farm made its first batch of cheese in March 2005. Michael and Emily currently gather about 175 pounds of milk from their small herd of exceptional dairy goats and from their neighbor's cows to make a raw-milk cheese.

A picture window from the driveway into the cheese room allows visitors to watch Michael stir the warm goat's milk and turn it into molds. From inside the house, views from every window look out onto the goats leaping up to attack the lower leaves of small maple trees. The goats keep the lower branches of the encroaching forest clear, and the Lees continue to clear most of the young trees for open pasture. Each year, as the farm grows and the land changes, so will the cheese. But for now, everything is new, green, and fresh, and the cheese that gracefully ages in the basement cave conveys a full flavor range of the seasonal pasture.

5. DANCING COW FARM

STEVE AND KAREN GETZ

237 Holstein Drive

Bridport, VT 05734

(802) 758-3267

www.dancingcowcheese.com

TYPE OF CHEESE: COW'S MILK

➤ **Menuet:** This semifirm, natural-rind is aged for a minimum of ninety days, resulting in buttery and sweet overtones.

➤ **Bourree:** This semisoft cheese is made with raw milk, washed with brine, and aged for at least sixty days. It has a smooth silky texture and a mild lingering taste.

➤ **Sarabande:** A washed-rind, pyramid, raw-milk cheese that is aged sixty days, this cheese is soft, slightly salty, and unctuous.

ABOUT THE CHEESE

All three types of Dancing Cow cheese are semifirm, aged, made with raw cow's milk, and have a natural rind. The drained curds are dusted with salt instead of immersed in brine, then left to cure for several days in a cool room to completely draw out the moisture. Then they enter the aging room for a minimum of sixty days, where they are carefully washed to keep a natural rind. The buttery farmstead cheese is best shaved into thin slices .

WHAT MAKES THIS CHEESE SPECIAL?

The lavish care of the animals is evident in the cheese, which is an extraordinary sunflower yellow, the result of natural betacarotenes spun directly from the suninfused fields into the cow's milk. Cheese is made only when the cows are eating grass, from May until November. During the winter months, they are fed hay (instead of silage) until they are ready to go out to pasture again. Warm milk from the small herd is piped warm, directly from the barn into the cheesemaking facility, and the resulting product is a pure farmstead cheese. As a new cheesemaking business, Dancing Cow Farm is still discovering new recipes and will continue to increase its production and repertoire.

HOW TO VISIT
Visitors are welcome and can view the cheesemaking every day from May until November. Call for times and exact dates.

DIRECTIONS
Take Route 22A to its intersection with Route 125 at Pratt's Store in Bridport. Turn left onto Route 125 West heading toward Lake Champlain. Travel 2.5 miles and turn right onto Holstein Drive. Drive to the end and park in the driveway of the farm.

Steve and Karen Getz, proud owners of Dancing Cow Farm, take a break in their cheese room.

ABOUT THE FARM

A WILD HEDGEROW FILLED WITH CHIRPING, prancing birds runs along the edges of the driveway leading up to Dancing Cow Farm. A tree house perched in the arms of a shade tree and a tire swing dangling below it is evidence of the family in residence; the tree house is also the perfect place to view the cows grazing across the farm's 240 lush acres. There is every reason for the cows (and the people) to be happy at Dancing Cow Farm, and when the animals turned out onto a new pasture, they can be seen kicking up their hind legs in what owners Karen and Steve Getz like to think of as a "dance of happiness."

In 2002, Karen and Steve gave up corporate careers in Pennsylvania and bought the classic farm, with its 150-year-old barns and simple farmhouse, with assistance from the Vermont Land Trust. After renovations, they bought a mixed herd of Jerseys from a farmer in St. Albans, crossbreeding them with Guernsey cows to develop a herd that encompasses the best of both breeds: good grazing abilities; strong, solid legs and hoofs; longevity; and excellent

After being pressed and removed from the cheese molds, wheels Dancing Cow's Menuet cheese will rest to form a dry exterior before being transferred to the aging cave.

milk. The Getzes now represent a new breed of dairy farmers who express their passion for the land and the animals through award-winning milk and a superbly crafted cheese.

Making the cows comfortable was foremost on the Getzes' minds. They created a system that pampers everyone, including Steve and Karen, who spend the morning in the barn, then the rest of the day managing the pastures and setting up new grazing paddocks.

The first thing Steve did was retrofit the milking parlor with a dry system, replacing the wet manure tracks with a thick bed of clean, dry wood chips. After milking each day, he shovels out any cow pies. The result is a spotless barn with minimal odor—so clean, Steve can tread through it in his Birkenstocks. A separate open-sided barn, erected closer to the lower fields, gives the cows a choice of living indoors or out, depending on the weather and the time of year.

The cows are milked once a day. To minimize handling, the milk flows directly from the cows in the milking parlor, to the cheese vat. Steve transfers the still-warm, certified-organic milk into the cheese room, where Karen or fellow cheesemaker Jeanne Finnerty stirs, separates, and presses cheese curds into molds.

An energy-efficient, temperature-balanced cheese aging room is located across the way in a separate outbuilding, insulated with 700 pounds of straw bales, reflective blankets, and a radiant cooling system that pumps fluid through the walls of the cave. An air exchanger keeps the cheese breathing clean air.

Though new to the Vermont cheese tradition, Karen and Steve are dancing as fast as they can, and their happily growing farm is flourishing.

Cheesemakers Jeanne Finnerty and Karen Getz of Dancing Cow Farm offers tasting samples.

6. CHAMPLAIN VALLEY CREAMERY

CARLETON YODER

11 Main Street

Vergennes, VT 05491

(802) 877-2950

www.cvcream.com

TYPE OF CHEESE: COW'S MILK

➤ **Cream Cheese:** This spreadable cheese is made with organic whole milk and cream. It is available plain and in a range of flavors, such as red onion, dill, and pepper.

➤ **Champlain Triple:** A small, round, soft-ripened cheese with a bloomy white rind is aged ten days before sale.

➤ **Ricotta:** Using the skim milk that is a byproduct of the cream cheese, this ricotta salata is a firm, crumbly, feta-like cheese. Sold primarily to restaurants.

ABOUT THE CHEESE

Drawing on his experience in the food industry, Carleton Yoder began making old-fashioned, organic cream cheese, which continues as his primary product. It is made without stabilizers or preservatives from cultured, fresh organic cow's milk and cream. The texture is creamy and slightly granular, similar to fresh goat cheese, yet with a distinctively sweet cow's milk flavor. This artisanal cheese is made from milk from a nearby farm. Each of the products is handmade in small batches, according to tried and true recipes.

WHAT MAKES THIS CHEESE SPECIAL?

With a background in food science and a degree in electrical engineering, Carleton Yoder brings a technical expertise to this cheesemaking venture, which involves science as well as art. The milk comes from a certified organic producer in Bridport, and the creamery is certified organic by Vermont Organic Farmers (VOF). Cream is separated from whole milk and heated to very low temperatures to retain flavor and natural minerals.

Thistle Hill Farm Tarantaise (cow's milk)

TOP PHOTO LEFT: *Shelburne Farms aged cheddar (cow's milk)* BOTTOM PHOTO LEFT: *Consider Bard-well Farm Mettowee chèvre (goat's milk)* ABOVE: *Collection of goat's milk cheese: (1) Blue Ledge Farm Chèvre (pepper variety), (2) Twig Farm Goat's Milk Tomme, (3) Vermont Butter & Cheese Company Bonne Bouche, (4) Lazy Lady Farm Les Pyramids, (5) Blue Ledge Farm La Luna*

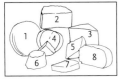

Collection of cow's milk cheeses: (1) Orb Weaver Farm Cave Aged, (2) Jasper Hill Farm Bayley Hazen Blue, (3) Thistle Hill Farm Tarantaise, (4) Taylor Farm Maple Smoked Gouda, (5) West River Creamery Middletown Tomme, (6) Jasper Hill Farm Constant Bliss, (7) Cobb Hill Ascutney Mountain, (8) Orb Weaver Farm Vermont Farmhouse Cheese

BELOW: *Blue Ledge Farm Lakes' Edge*
(goat's milk)

ABOVE: *Jasper Hill Farm Bayley Hazen Blue*
(cow's milk)

CLOCKWISE FROM TOP: *Willow Hill Farm Blue Moon, Alderbrook, and Vermont Brébis (sheep's milk)*

Orb Weaver Farm Cave Aged (left) and Vermont Farmhouse Cheese (right)

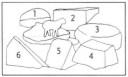

Collection of sheep's milk cheeses: (1) Hope Farm Sheep Cheese Pierce Hill, (2) Hope Farm Sheep Cheese Tomme de Brébis, (3) Willow Hill Farm Vermont Brébis, (4) Willow Hill Farm Alderbrook, (5) Willow Hill Farm Blue Moon, (6) Vermont Shepherd Tomme

HOW TO VISIT

Located in Vergennes, inside the Kennedy Brothers Factory Marketplace, the creamery facility has windows where visitors can watch the cheesemaking process. Products are available for sale in the marketplace gift shop from 9:30 A.M. to 5:30 P.M., seven days a week. You can also visit Carleton at the Middlebury Farmer's Market, where he sells flavor-of-the-week cream cheese, as well as all-natural cheesecakes.

DIRECTIONS

From Route 7, turn onto Route 22 towards Vergennes. The Kennedy Brothers Building is on the left. Champlain Valley Creamery is on the second floor.

ABOUT THE COMPANY

EVERY WEEK, Carleton Yoder lugs 1,000 pounds of milk up to the second floor of the Kennedy Brothers Building, built in the early 1900s, and then brings 200 pounds of packaged cheese back down the stairs. Carleton has created a dairy business without a farm. With his extensive knowledge of the food industry, he has managed to set up a facility that is still full of the romance that surrounds a cheesemaking business. Carleton, who has a background in winemaking, moved to Vermont in 1995 and worked for a business that made hard cider. After the business was sold, he switched over to making cheese at Shelburne Farms. In 2003, he ventured out on his own

Carleton Yoder makes organic cream cheese, ricotta, and Champlain Triple at Champlain Valley Creamery.

and launched Champlain Valley Creamery. With mini-mal start up costs, he managed to lease a former restaurant space, which already had a tile floor equipped with floor drain—a necessary element for draining whey from a cheesemaking room. He then purchased used cheesemaking equipment, including a 1952 De Laval cream separator that he bought in Canada. It separates the cream from the milk through a series of stacked discs; the whole milk is poured in the top, and centrifugal force separates the cream. The cream is transferred to a vat for pasteurizing, then to a blender for mixing and churning into cream cheese and other Champlain Valley Creamery products.

An old refrigerator serves as a temperature controlled aging cave for Champlain Valley Creamery's bloomy rind cheese.

7. ORB WEAVER FARM

MARJORIE SUSMAN AND MARIAN POLLACK

3406 Lime Kiln Road

New Haven, VT 05472

(802) 877-3755

www.orbweaverfarm.com

TYPE OF CHEESE: COW'S MILK

➤ **Vermont Farmhouse Cheese:** Moister than cheddar, this raw-milk cheese has a natural buttery color and smooth, creamy texture. Mildly flavored, it melts easily, for the ultimate grilled-cheese-and-tomato sandwich.

➤ **Cave Aged:** This cheese is made in much the same way as the Vermont Farmhouse Cheese, but is then transferred to the underground cave to age. The rind is left in a natural state to ripen into a smooth, tawny exterior. The result is a firm, buttery, and robust flavor with a complex array of nut and earthy notes, which have been picked up from the natural environment and the affinage process. Each cheese has a cow logo and lot number, which are imprinted into the curd when it is pressed into the molds.

ABOUT THE CHEESE

Since 1982, Orb Weaver Farm has been turning the high-butterfat milk from their small family of seven Jersey cows into a raw-milk cheese with an earthy, rich, and full-bodied flavor. The cows are left to graze on their own all summer, with minimal field rotations, and cheese is made from November to May, when owners organic market gardeners Marjorie Susman and Marian Pollack have more time to devote to cheese-making. The cows are fed a diet of organic hay and sweet-smelling grain during the winter, and the cheese is made in the nearby cheese room, using a process that takes three days to complete.

WHAT MAKES THIS CHEESE SPECIAL?

The creamy texture of the Vermont Farmhouse Cheese is the result of a time-tested recipe. Similar to a Havarti and Colby, the cheese is fragrant, with a sweet cow's milk flavor. The same recipe is aged in two ways: the younger cheese is waxed, then naturally aged in a temperature-controlled cooler just off the cheese room, while the cave-aged version is stored in a cave built with Lake Champlain stones from the neighboring town of Panton. The cave, which is warmer and more humid than the cooler, keeps the cheese ripening for up to one year and allows it to develop a clean, natural rind.

HOW TO VISIT
Marjorie and Marian are willing to impart their expertise with those who are interested, if time permits. Call ahead to check when they are available, as this is a working farm with no retail shop.

DIRECTIONS
Take Route 7 to New Haven, continue one mile up a hill, and turn onto Lime Kiln Road. Travel two miles to a four-way intersection, then continue straight for another mile to the second farmhouse on the right. The house is pale yellow with blue trim, and the underground cave, red barn, and silo are located down the hill.

ABOUT THE FARM

MARJORIE AND MARIAN HAVE INSPIRED countless cheesemakers since founding Orb Weaver in 1981. In 1977, they lived on a farm in Massachusetts and taught themselves how to make a farmhouse cheese in their kitchen. When Marjorie graduated from agricultural school, the two moved to Vermont, where they assumed everybody made cheese from their own cows. The two had been hired by a dairy farm in Monkton; Marjorie managed the farm, while Marian looked after the heifers, and they lived in a rundown farmworkers' house that has now become their own beautiful, handcrafted home.

The house, built in the 1780s, is perched on a hill with a great view of the fields and within a rural network other farmhouses along the dirt road, yet when they moved in, it had a leaky roof, aluminum siding, and no east-facing windows overlooking scenic fields. After a year, when the farm was up for sale, Marjorie and Marian purchased the house, thirty acres, and the run-down heifer barn, and bought their first cow, a Jersey named Sultana.

Marjorie Susman and Marian Pollack hold wheels of Orb Weaver cave-aged cheese. Each wheel is imprinted with the farm's cow logo, a lot number, and date.

In their home kitchen, they made cheese from Sultana's milk, but only for their own consumption. Eventually, the herd grew to fifty head, and milk was sold to a dairy cooperative. Orb Weaver Farm's reputation as one of the five top-producing farms in the nation was well known, and the dairy business was balanced with a large market garden. After almost fifteen years, the long hours and hard work to achieve this notoriety was wearing thin, and Marjorie and Marian were not convinced this was the way they wanted to spend their life. In 1995, they sold their prized herd, keeping only ten Jerseys, and began to make cheese with the four milking cows that remained. They now own 103 acres of lush fields and seven Jersey cows, and they produce close to 7,000 pounds of cheese per year. It's a small amount compared to some other cheesemakers, but it works for them, especially when offset by the four acres of market vegetables they continue to sell to local chefs and food co-ops.

The farm's namesake, orb weaver, is a common Vermont spider known for weaving an intricate, circular web; this web is a metaphor for the carefully structured nature of Marjorie

The aging cave at Orb Weaver farm was built into the hillside and constructed with Lake Champlain stones from the neighboring town of Panton.

and Marian's farm, the circular rhythm of the seasons, and all the connections that a self-contained farm can achieve. The two women make farming and cheesemaking look so easy, because they enjoy what they do and because they are highly organized.

It has taken them close to three decades to strike the right balance and learn how to work with the rhythms of nature. From May until the end of October, they tend to the vegetable-garden business. In November, after the cows give birth, they use the available milk for making cheese until May, when the cows dry off.

Over the years, Marjorie and Marian have held true to their commitment to local agriculture, growing their own food, and making their own bread. They take time to enjoy meals and the view from their screened-in porch on the east side of the house, overlooking the fields and the herd grazing happily on wild pasture all summer.

8. THREE OWLS SHEEP DAIRY

DAN HEWITT
4911 Route 100
Granville, VT 05747
(802) 767-4127
www.threeowlsfarm.com

TYPE OF CHEESE: SHEEP'S MILK, COW'S MILK

➤ **Three Owls Tomme:** This raw-milk, semihard, aged sheep cheese is pale yellow and lightly aromatic with sweet hints of hazelnut. The texture and lingering flavor notes vary greatly depending on its age.

➤ **Liberty Hill Blue:** Adapted from a Caledonian blue recipe, this crumbly, buttery blue cheese is mild with minimal veining. Made from cow's milk.

ABOUT THE CHEESE

Following the traditions of European cheesemakers, Dan Hewitt, cheesemaker and shepherd at Three Owls Sheep Dairy, makes small batches of a classic tomme—a mild-tasting, farmstead style, creamy sheep cheese that is brined and aged naturally in a temperature-controlled cooler right next to the cheese room. Liberty Hill Blue, made from milk from a neighboring farm, is a creamy, crumbly, natural-rind cheese with only a hint of blue vein that give it depth, rather than an overpowering character.

WHAT MAKES THIS CHEESE SPECIAL?

Making cheese only during the natural lactation season from May through the end of September, Three Owls Sheep Dairy currently produces about 2,000 pounds of sheep's milk cheese per year—not enough to sustain the farm as a full-time business, but enough to allow for experimentation and careful evaluation of the finished product. Commercial production began in 2003, and the young cheese is typically sold after three months of aging. While the young cheese is excellent, owner Dan Hewitt has recently held back some of the wheels to age for eight months, which will allow for the more complex flavors to develop.

HOW TO VISIT

Visitors can travel on scenic Route 100 down the Granville Gulf to find the retail store, located just outside the village of Granville and at local farmers markets. Cheese is made several days a week, and the process can be viewed through a glass window from the store. Call ahead for store

hours and cheesemaking days. Open May–Sept.

DIRECTIONS

Follow Route 100 south from Waitsfield or Warren, passing through Granville. Three Owls Sheep Dairy is about half a mile past the village on the right. Conversely, follow Route 100 north from Rochester and find Three Owls Sheep Dairy on the left, just before the village of Granville.

ABOUT THE FARM

IN 1994, WHEN DAN HEWITT; his wife, Daphne; and their two kids moved to Granville, (population 300) from his homeland, England, they were seeking solace from a crowded country. They chose eighty-eight acres in the heart of the Green Mountain National Forest, built a simple house, and settled into their new life. They named their farm Three Owls Sheep Dairy, a name derived from the Hewitt family coat of arms. While his wife pursued a master's degree in forestry from the University of Vermont, Dan built post-and-beam house frames, but both pined for open pasture, horses, and sheep.

In 1998, they purchased the only available flat land in Granville, conveniently located at the foot of their existing property. The land included an old farmhouse, several outbuildings, and a barn that was primarily used for raising heifers. Dan put his carpentry skills to work, revamped the barn, and built a first-rate cheesemaking room and retail shop.

They imported five East Friesian sheep from New Zealand to complement a small flock of mixed-breed local sheep. The East Friesian is reputedly the best sheep for milk production, but the flock contained only a few sheep that were good milk producers. Dan is still building his flock, breeding and keeping the better milking sheep. He considers not only the amount of milk each sheep produces, but also the shape of a sheep's udder, the animal's resistance to disease, and whether or not the sheep behaves in the milking parlor (no kicking!).

Dan's fascination with cheesemaking is due in part to his desire to recreate his childhood experiences and visits to his grandfather's farm. However, he is aware that the romance of cheese is in the finished, ready-to-eat wheels. Making cheese requires a few crucial decisions to create optimum conditions for the microorganisms that do the real work. He notes that "cheese is a living thing that you can't fully control, only guide in a direction."

Dan has taken a few cheesemaking courses in England and in Vermont. He has experimented with countless recipes to find just the

Shepherd / cheesemaker Dan Hewitt cuts samples of Three Owls Sheep Dairy's Liberty Hill Blue cheese.

right combination of heat, starter, and rennet and that makes the best use of his own farm conditions and the seasonal milk from his flock. With a natural cheesemaker's talent and good luck, he enjoys the process of making cheese, although he does not pursue it as his sole vocation. Taking time to build custom furniture balances his life.

Dan and Daphne are committed to raising happy animals—animals allowed as much freedom as possible to live their natural life, and eat the grass ruminants have evolved to eat. They try to tend the land in a way that leaves it in better condition than when they found it. They rotate the sheep to different grazing areas; mixing sheep with horses helps manage the parasites that both pick up naturally in the pasture, and encourages a diverse grass sward. Farming takes commitment, as does making cheese, and Three Owls Sheep Dairy is committed to both.

Wheels of sheep cheese in the temperature-controlled aging room at Three Owls Sheep Dairy.

CHAPTER 4

CHITTENDEN, GRAND ISLE, AND FRANKLIN COUNTIES

Shelburne • Milton • Alburg • Highgate Center • East Fairfield

THE NORTHERN COUNTIES OF VERMONT ENCOMPASS the best of several worlds: lush, open, grassy pasture; scenic mountain views; small towns; and a proximity to both Lake Champlain and the metropolitan area of Burlington. Bike paths wind along the lake's shoreline through Grand Isle and Chittenden counties, inviting riders to travel north and south in the summer months for long stretches along the water, around islands, and through spectacular farm country. Around the lake, the moist, fresh air benefits both people and agriculture, creating a landscape that is a refreshing change from the rest of the state's dense trees and mountainous terrain.

When visiting this region, it's best to start in Chittenden County, home of two of the cheesemakers in this chapter, each quite different from the other. As

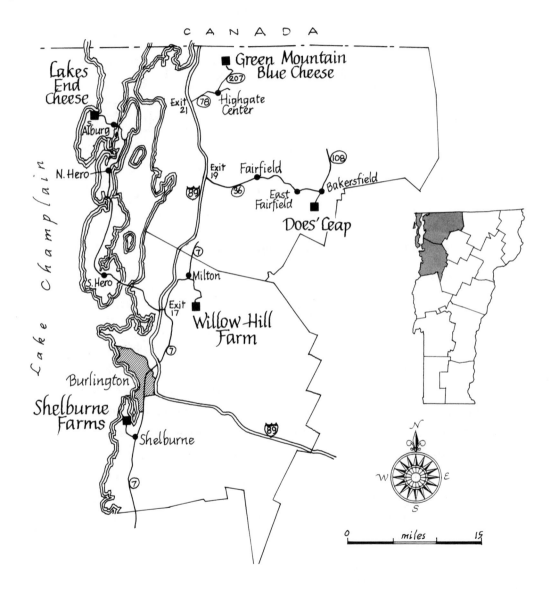

CANADA

Green Mountain
Blue Cheese

Lakes
End
Cheese

(207)

Exit
21
(78)
Highgate
Center

S.
Alburg

N. Hero

Exit
19
Fairfield
(108)

(89)
(36)
Bakersfield

East
Fairfield

Does' Leap

(7)

S. Hero
Milton

Exit
17
Willow Hill
Farm

(7)

Lake Champlain

Burlington

Shelburne
Farms
Shelburne

(89)

(7)

N

W   E

S

0   miles   15

a pioneer farmstead cheesemaker, **Shelburne Farms** (1) continues be a leading nonprofit environmental and educational organization. The farm was privately held until 1970, when the owning family turned the estate over to a public nonprofit preserve. Encompassing over 1,400 acres, hosting a range of enterprises, and driven by the core mission to cultivate conservation and demonstrate stewardship of the land and animals, Shelburne Farms has had a profound effect on the region. Today, visitors can experience a working-farm atmosphere, learn about cheesemaking, and stroll the grounds of this exquisite estate.

Farther north, in the small town of Milton, Willow Smart and David Phinney launched **Willow Hill Farm** (2) over a decade ago. They found an abandoned farm and began to raise vegetables while building a flock of sheep. It wasn't long before Willow became one of the leading artisan cheesemakers in the state, producing a wide range of unique and award-winning cheese which age to perfection in an earthen cave. Their farm and brand-new cheese-making facility is well worth a visit.

From Milton, cross the causeway into Grand Isle County, home to the Hero Islands, Isle La Motte, and Grand Isle—all situated in the northern Vermont section of Lake Champlain. Vistas of the lake rival the ocean views from Martha's Vineyard or other popular Atlantic vacation islands. Unlike the Vineyard, however, Lake Champlain has only recently been discovered by tourists. Stretches of flat, open farmland abound, all with a cornucopia of wildflowers and natural grasses enlivened by the moisture from the lake. Here you will find **Lakes End Cheeses** (3), the only remaining full-time dairy farm of six that once lined the North Shore Road, overlooking Isle La Motte. The lush landscape enhances the flavor of the farm's goat's milk chèvre, and the moisture of the lakefront air creates the unique affinage in the farmstead cheeses.

Continue north until just shy of the Canadian border, and turn east at Alburg to Highgate Center, home of **Green Mountain Blue Cheese** (4). Here is true dairy country, with silos, metal-roofed utility buildings, and large open-sided barns. Generations of farm families own large tracts of land, and town life is simple, yet thriving due to nearby tourist areas and the success of hard-working family farms. Like many in this region, the Boucher family emigrated from Canada and created several large, thriving dairy farms that have sustained this area for many years.

East Fairfield and **Does' Leap** (5) are located to the west, in the heart of Franklin County. Although only fifty miles from Burlington, the farm seems too remote and tranquil for a young couple. But the diversity and affordability of the land make this location ideal for an expanding herd of goats and for making high-quality chèvre.

Farmers' markets in this northern region are popular, and a diverse group of farmers attend regularly, since the markets are reliable places to sell meat, eggs, vegetables, and cheese. All the cheesemakers in this chapter are active members of their local farmers' markets where their cheese is available.

1. SHELBURNE FARMS

1611 Harbor Road

Shelburne, VT 05482

www.shelburnefarms.org

TYPE OF CHEESE: COW'S MILK

➤ **Six- to Nine-Month Cheddar:** Creamy and mild, this cheese is ideal for those with more conservative palates.

➤ **One-Year Cheddar:** This classic New England cheddar has a pleasantly sharp, well-balanced flavor.

➤ **Two-Year Cheddar:** After two years, the characteristic flavors of cheddar become more pronounced. This cheese is known for its bold taste, full-bodied aroma, and dry, crumbly texture.

➤ **Clothbound Cheddar:** Hand-wrapped in cheesecloth and rubbed with lard to preserve moisture and encourage good molds, these truckles (a traditional English term) are round cylinders that are taller than they are wide. Following a centuries-old English tradition, this cheddar is aged for more than a year to enhance its earthy flavor and golden color. Only a handful are made each day, so quantities are limited.

ABOUT THE CHEESE

In the 1950s, the owners of Shelburne Farms decided to raise Brown Swiss cows because of the breed's hardiness and temperament. Today the farm has 225 registered Brown Swiss, of which 125 are milking cows and 100 are young stock. Each cow will produce an average of fifty pounds of milk per day. Brown Swiss milk has a higher butterfat content than that of most other breeds, which translates into an especially creamy cheddar. Every day, between 5,000 and 7,000 pounds of milk is transported from the milking parlor to the cheese room to be turned into 550 to 800 pounds of cheese. Over 130,000 pounds of cheese is produced each year, and all of the proceeds are used to support the farm's educational mission.

WHAT MAKES THIS CHEESE SPECIAL?

Cheesemaker Jaime Yturriondobeitia follows a succession of talented cheesemakers, each of whom taught the next in the art of cheddaring. Jaime's background in biotechnology and chemistry brings science and precision to the established methods. Her goal is to continue to perfect the traditional recipe for the famous two-year-old cheddar, developing systems that will take it to a sophisticated level without sacrificing the qualities that make the cheese special. She understands how to work with the changes in each day's milk—determined by what the cows eat, the weather, and the grazing conditions—to achieve a product that consistently wins awards of excellence from the American Cheese Society.

HOW TO VISIT

Visitors to Shelburne Farms are welcome to view cheesemaking from the windows outside the cheese room from mid-May to mid-October. In keeping with the mission at Shelburne Farms, detailed photographs and descriptions educate visitors on the step-by-step process of cheesemaking.

DIRECTIONS

Take Route 7 to Shelburne Center, turn west at the light, and drive two miles to the entrance to Shelburne Farms. Day-pass admission and property tours are available at the Welcome Center, located at the farm's entrance, from mid-May through mid-October.

ABOUT THE FARM

THE STORY BEHIND SHELBURNE FARMS dates back to 1886, when Dr. William Seward and Lila Vanderbilt Webb acquired the farm on the shores of Lake Champlain as a summer residence and with the desire to establish a model agricultural farm. Their vision was enhanced by the efforts of two of the most prominent planners in the country at the time, architect Robert H. Robertson and landscape architect Frederick

Law Olmsted, Sr. While Robertson designed the buildings, Olmstead focused on the layout of the farm, fields, and forest. By 1902, the 3,800-acre farm was renown as an agricultural-innovation mecca, complete with a Hackney horse-breeding enterprise and a magnificent family residence. An annual harvest of 1,500 tons of hay and 12,000 bushels of grain supported a large flock of Southdown sheep, Jersey dairy cattle, Hackney horses, pigs, poultry, and gaming pheasants. The farm produced enough vegetables, milk, pork, fruit, and eggs to support the Webb residence, including staff and farm help, and an abundance was still shipped to markets in New York City.

Cheesemaking at Shelburne Farms takes place in the massive, beautifully restored barn.

The grand scale of the farm and agricultural venture, however, could not be sustained, and from 1910 through the 1950s, farming operations shrank. The farm remained within the Webb family, who struggled to maintain it until 1972. That year, Shelburne Farms was re-created as a membership-supported, nonprofit educational center practicing rural land use that is environmentally, economically, and culturally sustainable.

Jump ahead to the 1980s, when Alec and Marshall Webb, great-grandsons of the founders, began to restore the farms original agricultural pursuits. They researched the possibility of adding a milk-bottling plant as an additional source of revenue for the farm, but faced with the potential liability issues that surrounded raw milk, they instead turned to making

Shelburne Farms' head cheesemaker Jaime Yturriondobeitia (left) and her assistant cut the curds of a vat of set milk.

Today at the FARMYARD

10:00	Good Morning!
10:30	Chicken Parade
11:00	Milk a Cow
11:30	Meet Freckles the Llama
12:00	Get in the Garden
12:30	Milk a Goat
1:00	Bottle Feeding
1:30	Brush a Donkey
2:00	Milk a Cow
2:30	Meet a Goat Kid
3:00	Meet a Calf
3:30	Farm Chores
4:00	Milk a Cow by Machine

A signboard lists the daily educational events at Shelburne Farms.

cheese. Bill Clapp became the first cheesemaker at Shelburne Farms and traveled to England with Marshall to learn how to make cheese.

The dairy at Shelburne Farms is one of the finest examples of sustainable agriculture at work, and it is the basis for the cheesemaking operation. Of the 1,400 acres that remain part of the estate, about 500 are reserved for grazing the Brown Swiss herd. The milking parlor, constructed in 1995, complements the system by quickly milking cows and returning them to the pasture. The parlor has an efficient design where sixteen cows line up along one side of the pit where the milker works. Two people currently milk about eighty cows an hour, taking extra time to prep the cows to ensure the highest quality milk for cheese production.

The main residence has been meticulously restored and serves as an inn and restaurant during the summer. When you see the view of the lake from the house though the tiered gardens, it is easy to imagine the excitement and unlimited enthusiasm Seward and Webb must have felt when they created Shelburne Farms over one hundred years ago. Thanks to the diligence of family members and the nonprofit organization, most of the farm buildings are rehabilitated and preserved, the agricultural landscape restored, and the remaining acreage permanently protected with conservation easements. Both the land and buildings are on the National Register of Historic Places.

2. WILLOW HILL FARM

WILLOW SMART AND DAVID PHINNEY

313 Hardscrabble Road

Milton, VT 05468

(802) 893-2963

www.sheepcheese.com

TYPE OF CHEESE: SHEEP'S MILK, COW'S MILK

➤ **Alderbrook:** This semi-ripened, soft sheep cheese is buttery with an herby finish, and it can be further ripened into a runny, earthy delicacy.

➤ **Autumn Oak:** This smooth, creamy, natural-rind sheep cheese is reminiscent of wild woodland mushrooms.

➤ **Blue Moon:** A creamy, mild sheep's milk blue cheese that begins with a bit of tang and finishes with buttery earthiness. It takes its name from the fact that it is made "once in a blue moon," when the farm's ewes' milk is richest.

➤ **Cobble Hill:** This Brie-shaped cheese is buttery, creamy, and has notes of mushroom. It is named after an unusual rock outcropping located on the farm.

➤ **Fernwood:** This rare, unctuous, soft-ripened cheese made from the buttery-rich milk of Brown Swiss and Dutch Belted cows. It is aged at least sixty days in an underground cave.

➤ **La Fluerie:** This disc-shaped, bloomy-rind, cow's milk cheese is like a mini Camembert. Made from rich Brown Swiss cows' milk, it is creamy and nutty, yet earthy.

➤ **Mountain Tomme:** This blend of sheep's and cow's milk is made in the style of Pyrenees' mountain cheeses and made only when the cows and sheep are grazing in the lush hillside pastures. Aged at least five months, it is both woodsy and buttery and has a hazelnut-like finish.

➤ **Summertomme:** Introduced in 2001, this small round is made in the style of Brin d'Amour, but with a slightly different herb crust. It has a Provençal

nature, with rich buttery notes and an almost floral finish.
➤ **Vermont Brébis:** A small, round wheel, this sheep cheese tastes of herbs and mushrooms. It is runny when ripe.

ABOUT THE CHEESE
Cheesemaker Willow Smart has developed nine types of cheese to reflect the best of the rich, creamy milk produced by their flock of 150 sheep and six Brown Swiss and Dutch Belted Cows. Her husband, David Phinney, is the herdsman, and he tends to the farm chores and milking. Cheese is produced daily during the months when the sheep and cows are producing milk, May through February.

Willow Hill Farm offers four raw-milk cheeses, which are held for the required minimum of sixty days or cave aged for longer; five pasteurized-milk cheeses, sometimes sold as young, bloomy, soft cheese; and an award-winning sheep's milk yogurt. The farm produces close to 8,000 pounds of cheese per year and, with the recent addition of a new cheesemaking facility, hopes to increase production.

WHAT MAKES THIS CHEESE SPECIAL?
A finishing process that takes place in the earthen caves and Willow's confidence in the cheesemaking process are what set Willow Hill Farm's cheese apart from other American cheeses and put it on par with European counterparts. In true farmstead-cheese style, the sheep's milk is lovingly toted from the barn up the hill to the cheesemaking parlor. Once the cheese is made, it is carefully placed in the nearby natural cave to age. An exposed bedrock wall exudes moss rootlets and tiny water drops, creating natural humidity, which, along with the cave's fluctuating geothermal temperature, gives an earthy quality to the cheese. Willow Hill's bloomy-rind sheep's milk cheeses are cured about fourteen days (though each one is different) and reach their peak in three to four weeks after the date they are made.

The new cheesemaking facility uses a European-style method, which requires minimal milk handling. Fresh milk is brought to the cheese house from the milking barn and is gravity fed into the cheesemaking vat, located on a level below.

HOW TO VISIT

Visitors are welcome to view the cheese-making process. Cheesemaking takes place every day, and cheese is for sale in the self-serve retail shop located at the farm. Call ahead for best times to visit.

DIRECTIONS

Take Interstate 89 north to exit 17 (the Milton exit). Drive four miles to Milton Center. Turn right onto Main Street. After the railroad tracks, take the second right onto East Road. Travel for 0.75 miles, then take a left onto Hardscrabble Road. Drive 1.25 miles uphill to the Willow Hill Farm sign on the right, before the green barn. Drive up the long driveway to the new cheese-making building.

ABOUT THE FARM

WILLOW SMART AND DAVID PHINNEY purchased their property in Milton, David's hometown, in 1991, after searching all over Vermont for a farm. They named it Willow Hill Farm, in part for Willow herself, but also for the abundance of willow that grows in the wet pockets all around the farm. The former dairy farm had been abandoned years before, and the land and buildings were badly neglected. The farm consisted of 478 acres, only 50 acres of which was open land, and a barn, which burned down the fifth year after David and Willow started farming. (They lost everything, including their tractors, but not their animals.) They rebuilt the barn on the original footprint, at the foot of the driveway.

Their farming life began with five acres of organic vegetables, a pick-your-own berry business, and two greenhouses where they raised starter plants for local gardeners. They slowly added sheep, mostly to keep the scrub low, but also to sell for meat and wool.

Owner/cheesemaker Willow Smart stands outside the cave where her bloomy-rind sheep's milk cheeses are aged.

In 1996, Willow, who has always loved cheese, started experimenting with cheese recipes in a small cheesemaking room set up at the barn. These experiments fueled her desire to learn more and to buy sheep for milking. She contacted David and Cindy Major at Vermont Shepherd and for two years produced cheese for their brand, while building her own flock of East Friesian–Suffolk cross sheep and experimenting with her own style of sheep's milk cheese.

In 1999, Willow and David cleared trees from a knoll and excavated a cave for ripening the cheese. The stones removed from the site were used to form a retaining wall and exterior for the cave. They gave the front of the cave several small windows to provide natural light in the wrapping and shipping room. The cave also has two affinage chambers, where the cheese receives a natural, earth-ripened finish. The unique cave is perhaps the only one in the country that has exposed bedrock forming its back wall. A draining, open bedrock wall provides natural humidity and moisture, creating ideal conditions for the affinage of the cheese. A door separates the bedrock from the cheese, and if the cave gets too moist, the door can be shut. When the weather is dry during the summer, an artificial fogger is triggered to provide moisture.

Willow Hill Farm's nine cheeses, each named after the changing seasons and geographic characteristics of the farm, all have won numerous awards. Willow's recipes are created by the characteristics of the milk, and she makes the most of the rich flavor and butterfat content that only sheep's milk can provide. In 2006, Willow Hill Farm celebrated its tenth year of cheesemaking and put the finishing touches on a new cheese facility that is closer to the cave in the middle of the farm.

3. LAKES END CHEESES

JOANNE AND ALTON JAMES

212 West Shore Road
Alburg, VT 05440
(802) 796-3730
www.lakesendcheeses.com

TYPE OF CHEESE: GOAT'S MILK, COW'S MILK

➤ **Champlain Chèvre:** This soft, spreadable chèvre is made from lightly pastured milk.

➤ **Misty Cove:** This alpine-style raw-milk tomme is made from cow's and goat's milk. It is naturally aged to form a natural rind; a firm, creamy interior; and a mild flavor.

➤ **Harbor Light:** A goat's and cow's milk Brie made in twenty-five gallon batches, this soft-ripened cheese is aged for ten weeks to develop a soft interior and gentle white mold. Because of the farm's close proximity to the lake, the rind is naturally dotted with spores indigenous to the region.

➤ **James Bay:** Made from a combination of cow's and goat's milk and aged for sixty days, this firm, naturally ripened cheese has a light color and flavor.

ABOUT THE CHEESE

Lakes End hand-makes certified-organic, raw-milk cheese in small batches. It took four years of making cheese in her kitchen before Joanne James was confident enough to apply for a cheese license and begin producing her first product: a fresh, soft, spreadable chèvre, which she sold at her farmstand along with fresh eggs and chocolate. This small, diversified farm also combines pure cow's milk from its Jersey herd with goat's milk to create several complex blended cheeses.

WHAT MAKES THIS CHEESE SPECIAL?

Since this is a small one-person operation, cheese is handmade in a home-style kitchen with professional equipment and the herds get extra special attention. Certified-organic hay is harvested from surrounding fields, and no silage is fed to the goats or cows throughout the year. The animals are fed a minimal amount of grain year-round, which guarantees they will get most of their nutrition from the pasture. Pasture grazing boosts the quality of their milk, and that quality is ultimately reflected in the cheese.

HOW TO VISIT

Farmstand hours are Monday through Saturday, 10 A.M. to 4 P.M., Memorial Day through Labor Day. Cheese is in the outdoor cooler. If it is cheesemaking day, visitors can watch the work from the glass window into the cheese room.

DIRECTIONS

From Burlington, take Route 7 Route 2 north, passing North Hero to reach South Alburg. Turn left on West Shore Road and go for 2.5 miles. Signs for eggs, cheese, and chocolate will be posted at the end of the driveway, on the right side.

ABOUT THE FARM

JOANNE AND ALTON JAMES have the best of two worlds: twenty-eight acres of flat pasture on which to graze their animals and, across the road, a house with wrap-around porch, perched above the northernmost section of Lake Champlain. But they have worked hard to earn this slice of heaven and find time only during the winter months to relax and enjoy the view. Judging by the price of farmland on this small island, the pressure to stay agricultural is hard to do, especially with lakefront property.

Lakes End Cheeses is only one enterprise that Joanne has created over the past two decades, mostly as a way to keep busy and to supplement the income from her husband's full-time job as a home heating and plumbing specialist. Alton's grandfather bought the 180-acre farm in the 1940s and raised cows, selling milk to the St. Albans Cooperative Creamery.

Alton grew up on the farm, as his parents continued the dairy-farming tradition. When the barn burned to the ground in the mid-1960s, the cost to rebuild it was too high, so Joanne and Alton decided to quit farming.

With fairness in mind, the family split the land into strips; each segment is approximately 250 feet wide and has both pasture and lake front property. Newly married and with little money, Joanne and Alton purchased one slice and set out to pay the mortgage in various ways. Alton worked off the farm, while Joanne raised two children and grew an expansive garden, canning food for the winter and

Signs for eggs, cheese, and candy are mark the driveway leading to the James farm in South Alburg.

making preserves and pickles for a roadside farmstand that was open during the summer months.

Tourists flocked to the stand to buy her preserves. In the mid-1980s, she started selling hand-dipped chocolates and, by 1995, farmstead cheese. Little by little, she and Alton added farm animals. First, they bought a flock of chickens in order to sell fresh eggs; in 1991, they purchased forty Toggenburg goats for the milk, and in 1999, they added two Jersey cows to blend the milk for Lakes End cheese. Every year, they raise two hogs on the whey left over from the cheesemaking, and sell the meat at the farmer's market, as well as from a freezer at the farm.

4. GREEN MOUNTAIN BLUE CHEESE

DAWN MORIN-BOUCHER AND DANIEL BOUCHER
2183 Gore Road
Highgate Center, VT 05459
(802) 868-4193

TYPE OF CHEESE: COW'S MILK

➤ **Boucher Blue/Vermont Blue Cheese:** This blue is smooth, very creamy, and mild, with undertones of chestnuts, sweet hay, and truffles. It is based on the French *Fourme d'Ambert* and unique to the farm.

➤ **Gore-Dawn-Zola:** Made in the Gorgonzola style, tangy, this cheese is sharp and crumbly with a bitter chocolate aroma. The surface is scraped down before wrapping and further aging in a cheese cellar.

➤ **Brother Laurent:** This washed-rind, French, Muenster-style cheese named for Daniel's uncle, Holy Brother Laurent Boucher, who made frequent trips from Montreal to the farm. It is very aromatic, dense, and tangy.

ABOUT THE CHEESE

Before launching Green Mountain Blue in 1998, Dawn Morin-Boucher conducted market research in her kitchen and at the supermarket. In the stores, blue cheese was the one cheese that had the best turnover. It required a minimum amount of equipment to produce (no heavy presses for draining the whey), and no curds needed washing. And since the mold was introduced from specific cultures, the turning and affinage were less prone to chance compared to other types of natural-ripened and rind cheeses.

Boucher Blue is made once a week from fresh milk pumped directly from the barn into the nearby cheese room. The full cheesemaking process, including the time after the cheese is pressed into a mold, drained, and left to dry in one of the three aging rooms, takes two days to complete. The cheese is hand-salted twice in the first week, turned every day, and hand-pierced after the first week with a knitting needle to create holes where oxygen can encourage the blue mold to grow. The aging rooms' humidity levels are kept constant, and plenty of air circulates to create an evenly ripened cheese. The other cheeses are also handmade in small batches with the same level of care.

WHAT MAKES THIS CHEESE SPECIAL?

Only one year after Green Mountain Blue Cheese began making cheese, Boucher Blue won a third-place ribbon in the American Cheese Society awards. The cheese always sells out quickly, and aged inventory is a rarity. Production continues to grow 20 percent every year, and during the summer of 2006, Dawn's fourteen-year-old niece joined her as an *affineuse* in training.

"She's a natural," says Dawn. "Affinage is all down to the hands and skill of the person handling the cheeses, and I am proud to say that with minimal instruction she

has been able to make great improvements in our blue cheeses."

Dawn is also proud of the way her cheeses' natural rinds are developing closer to the European ideal. These rinds develop naturally from the environment; no cultures need to be added to produce or encourage them.

HOW TO VISIT

Visitors are welcome anytime; they can watch the cheesemaking process or purchase cheese from a self-serve refrigerator in the entrance room of the cheese room.

DIRECTIONS

From Interstate 89 North, take exit 21. Take a right at the end of the ramp and go 2.5 miles to Highgate Center. Just after the fire department on the right, there is a black state sign that directs you to take a left onto Route 207, which is also called Gore Road, and travel north 2.5 miles. Green Mountain Blue Cheese and its barn are set back from the road, but clearly marked in big lettering that says "Boucher Family Farm."

ABOUT THE FARM

JUST MINUTES AWAY FROM THE CANADIAN BORDER, Lake Champlain and the Missisquoi Bay, the Boucher family farm covers 1,200 acres and is one in a series of orderly, large-scale farms along Route 207. The Boucher family farm is distinguished by a series of five brown barns connected by a circular driveway and has three farmhouses for the Bourcher brothers and their parents.

This northwestern section of Vermont is full of the history of the French farmers who settled the region. During the French and Indian Wars, one Boucher ancestor, Pierre Boucher, took control of Fort Trois Rivieres (in what is now Quebec) and made peace with the Iroquois; the Quebec city of Boucherville was subsequently named in his honor. A line of Bouchers has been active in Vermont agriculture ever since Rene Boucher moved his family to the area to farm in the 1940s. His son Gilbert, the youngest of eleven brothers and sisters, took over all responsibilities at age fourteen. Two of Gilbert's four sons, Daniel and Denis, twelfth-generation farmers, took over the daily operations at the Boucher family farm in 1991 and diversified the operation to include raising calves, beef cattle, and pigs; growing grain; milking 120 Holstein cows; and selling eggs, turkey, and cheese.

Daniel married Dawn Morin-Boucher, who had just finished college and was working in a job off the farm when the brothers acquired the property. Dawn adapted to life on the farm, blending her off-farm work with various skills, including preserving food from her large garden, baking bread, and brewing beer

The freestanding cheesemaking facility and cheese room at the Boucher family farm

Row upon row of Green Mountain Blue Cheese's signature product ripen gently in the aging room.

and making wine. In true farm-wife style, she taught herself how to make cheese. Cheese-making developed into a passion and seemed like an excellent way to move onto the farm full time. Dawn borrowed start-up money from her in-laws in 1997 to establish Green Mountain Blue Cheese and focused on making it a success.

The cheesemaking company is a separate entity from the working family farm, but Dawn makes the most of the convenient location next door to the milking parlor. One day a week, the milk from the herd is pumped into the storage tanks and cheesemaking begins. Only 3 percent of the farm's total milk production goes towards producing the cheese, but Green Mountain Blue Cheese has become a valuable and integral part of the overall farm operation.

5. DOES' LEAP

KRISTAN DOOLAN AND GEORGE VANVLAANDEREN

1703 Route 108 South

East Fairfield, VT 05448

(802) 827-3046

TYPE OF CHEESE: GOAT'S MILK

➤ **Fresh Chèvre:** Certified organic, available plain or rolled in dried *herbes de Provence*, this fresh pasteurized-milk chèvre has subtle floral and woodsy qualities. It has an especially sweet, fragrant appeal.

➤ **Feta:** This fresh raw-milk cheese is marinated in salt brine and minimally aged.

➤ **Caprella:** A milky, buttery round made from pasteurized milk and aged naturally for three to four weeks. With a soft white mold outside and a creamy interior, ripens from outside in.

➤ **Trappist Style:** An aged tomme with full flavor notes, this washed-curd cheese is made from unpasteurized milk and aged four months. It is made in April and May, when the milk is most vibrant, and left to age until late summer.

ABOUT THE CHEESE

Does' Leap makes four types of certified organic cheese from the milk of the farm's own goats. Made in small batches by hand, Does' Leap cheeses capture the essence of a wild Vermont summer, since the herd is left to pasture in a largely wooded lot. Careful field rotations, dictated by an aerial map, make sure that the goats are well fed and the young shoots from wild grasses, flowers, and shrubs are allowed to regrow rapidly. As a result, the animals' milk produces fresh cheese with a light, seasonal, woodsy essence.

WHAT MAKES THIS CHEESE SPECIAL?

Making cheese is a ritual that flows easily and is a way of life that sustains this young family. Kristan and George currently produce about 6,000 pounds of certified organic cheese, and in 2006 they hope to double the size of their cheese room to accommodate more production. Kristan is the primary cheesemaker and a natural herdswoman; she makes Does' Leap cheese with the skill that comes from experience and a natural intuition.

HOW TO VISIT

The Does' Leap farm isn't currently set up for showing the cheesemaking process to visitors, but cheese is often available at the farm. Call ahead for availability. The company's cheese is also available at the Burlington farmers' market in City Hall Park during the summer and at select restaurants and retailers in the area.

DIRECTIONS

From Burlington, take Interstate 89 North and get off at exit 19, the St. Albans exit. Take a right off the exit, go 0.5 mile, and take a right onto Route 36 going east. Go 16 miles, then take a right onto Route 108 going south, and go 1.8 miles. The farm's driveway is on the left.

ABOUT THE FARM

THE LONG, WINDING GRAVEL DRIVEWAY at Does' Leap farm is marked by a single black mailbox. On the bumpy ride up to the top, you'll pass a small flock of young goat kids and a rustic cabin before reaching the main house. Two border collies, a sheepdog, and a small terrier greet visitors, but the goats are nowhere in sight. An independent bunch, they are off foraging on the farm's 130 acres (mostly in the woods behind the barn). An electric fence surrounds the property mostly to protect the house, rather than to restrain the goats.

Soon after Kristan Doolan and George VanVlaanderen earned their master's degrees in agriculture from the University of Maine in 1997, they bought property in East Fairfield. Kristan grew up in nearby Fletcher, while George's family lives in southern Vermont. The

Zoe Van Vlaanderen cuts into a wheel of fresh Caprella cheese at Does' Leap Farm. Also featured on the cheese plate are a chèvre rolled in herbes de Provence *and a wedge of an aged tomme.*

Franklin County land was affordable and located within a fifty miles of Burlington.

For economy, Kristan and George made their home in a yurt, a nomadic, Mongolian structure that is more stable than a tent, and they depended on a wood stove for heat. Determined to start farming as soon as possible, they raised a barn and purchased their initial flock: three Nubian goats that would be fed only organic grains. Both worked off the farm at first, structuring their work schedule to be able to milk the goats twice a day and to make cheese at night or in the early morning hours in a makeshift kitchen. Whenever they could squeeze in the time, they took cheesemaking classes with the legendary Kathy Bis, Margaret Morris, and University of Vermont's professor Paul Kinsteadt. In 1998, they finished building their own milking parlor and cheese room.

Kristan and George became licensed cheesemakers in 1999 and have since built a post-and-beam house that connects to the cheese room via a hallway. Aging caves are located in the basement beneath the family kitchen. The goal was to keep the whole operation under one roof; though the residence and cheesemaking facilities are separated by a series of doors and hallways, it is easy for Kristan and George's two young children to travel back and forth without going outdoors.

Their herd has grown to forty-three mixed Alpine-Nubian goats, which Kristan and

George consider to be the best blend of breeds. Alpines are hearty and don't mind changes; the Nubians are a bit more anxious, but their milk is sweet and high in butterfat. The goats at Does' Leap are happy to forage on a variety of native grass, sweet clover, and tree boughs, and while they are mostly wild, they are also tightly managed. Kristan and George used an aerial photograph of their farm to divide the property into thirty-two numbered paddocks; they rotate the flock through the paddocks five times throughout the year. This rotation plan allows for a healthy diversity of plants and allows the shrubs and young trees to sprout new growth before the animals return.

Kristan Doolan and George Van Vlaanderen, owners of Does' Leap, and some of their Alpine-Nubian goats

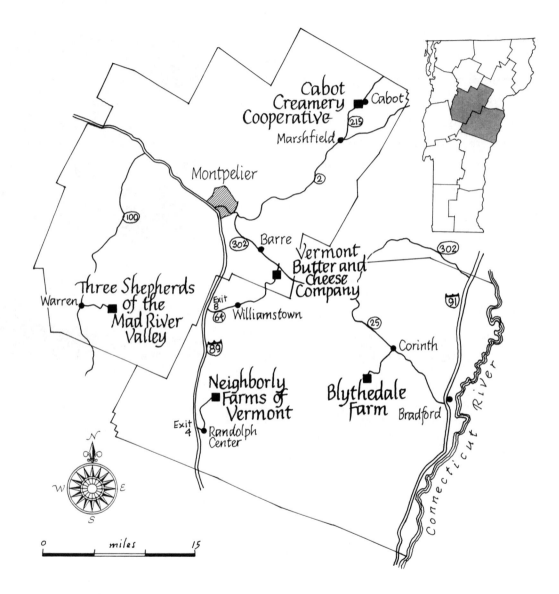

Cabot
Creamery
Cooperative ■ Cabot

215

Marshfield •

Montpelier

2

100

302

Barre

302

91

Vermont
Butter and
Cheese
Company

Three Shepherds
of the
Mad River
Valley

Exit
8

64

Williamstown

25

Corinth

Warren •

89

Neighborly
Farms of
Vermont

Blythedale
Farm

Bradford

Exit
4 • Randolph
Center

Connecticut River

N
W   E
S

0   miles   15

CHAPTER 5

WASHINGTON AND ORANGE COUNTIES

Warren • Randolph Center • Corinth • Websterville • Cabot

ORANGE COUNTY COVERS THE AREA OF VERMONT THAT borders New Hampshire along the upper Connecticut River. The city of Barre, the largest city in this predominately rural area, is situated where three brooks come together in a single valley. In the early days, the brooks supplied power for settlers' gristmills and sawmills and, later on, for the granite sheds and other manufacturers. Barre is the center of Vermont's granite industry and home to the Rock of Ages quarries. The fame of this vast deposit of granite, which some geologists say is four miles long, two miles wide, and ten miles deep, soon spread to Europe and Canada, prompting a large influx of workers from Italy, Scotland, Spain, and Scandinavia in the 1800s. Although granite mining became the major industry for this region, these new immigrants also raised sheep on the hilly terrain.

Central Vermont wasn't created to host visitors, yet the region's historic buildings are living museums, open to the public and part of everyday life.

Simple houses, functional barns, rural valleys, rolling hills, and occasional looming piles of granite slabs, stacked behind abandoned quarries, define this area, which is both sparse and scenic. Driving the narrow winding roads, one rarely passes other cars, but the occasional tractor moves slowly down the road to a hayfield. Grange halls, town halls, town greens, and the general stores form the foundations in the village and the structure that maintains vibrant communities.

Geographically, this sparse yet scenic area, largely untouched by development, captures the essence of Vermont. Traditional farms dot the landscape, and people work close to home and close to the land. No large mountain range defines this area, yet many rolling hills prevent long stretches of open land; the farmland is rocky, and the soil is thin. Only the most resourceful and hard-working farmers still work the land.

All of the cheesemakers in Washington and Orange Counties are dedicated to preserving a way of life that conforms to the simplicity of the landscape, while keeping them connected to the land. They tend small herds with meticulous care, and cheesemaking fits into their grander plan to keep the Vermont family farm alive. **Three Shepherds of the Mad River Valley** (1) in Warren is on the northern edge of the Green Mountain National Forest. Due to an embargo on their flock of East Friesian sheep, the company currently purchases milk from nearby farms in order to make its artisanal cheese. **Neighborly Farms of Vermont** (2) in Randolph Center is just off Interstate 89. Here the landscape shifts dramatically from mountains back into farm country, and relatively flat, open fields with grazing cows can be seen in all directions. A swath of dairy farms is located in this valley, sharing fences and jockeying for hayfields.

Blythedale Farm (3) in Corinth will probably never be a tourist destination, yet owners Tom and Becky Loftus like it this way. They rarely leave the farm, and their simple farmhouse is only a few steps away from the cheese house and the milking barn. The Jersey cows are good company and produce high-butterfat milk for their signature soft-ripened cheese that travels to markets all over the United States. The cheesemaking business allows the Loftus family to continue a lifestyle and tradition that this farm has known for 200 years.

A short hike up Route 302 is the **Vermont Butter & Cheese Company** (4). Located in an industrial park, the company has no goats, yet owners Allison Hooper and Bob Reese work closely with thirty-one Vermont goat farmers, who provide milk for their product. The final stop is **Cabot Creamery** (5), located in the quintessential small village of Cabot. When visiting, be sure to take the excellent tour to watch the cheesemaking process and fill your cooler with Vermont's best-known cheese.

Cheesemaker Bessie Sandberg heating milk to make Camembert and Brie cheese at Blythedale Farm.

1. THREE SHEPHERDS OF THE MAD RIVER VALLEY

LINDA AND LARRY FAILLACE

42 Roxbury Mountain Road

Warren, VT 05674

(802) 496-4559

www.rootswork.org

TYPE OF CHEESE: SHEEP'S MILK, COW'S MILK

➤ **Aurora:** Made from raw cow's milk, this mellow, cave-aged, semihard cheese is noted for the beautiful color of its washed rind.

➤ **Vermont Brabander:** This natural-rind, raw cow's milk cheese has a bold nutty flavor and a crumbly texture.

➤ **Montagne:** Like an authentic peasant's cheese, this raw sheep's milk is hand-pressed.

➤ **Cosmos:** This soft-ripened, raw sheep's milk cheese is infused with herbs.

ABOUT THE CHEESE

The original goal of this small farm was to produce pure sheep's cheese; however, with the loss of their sheep, the Faillace family has managed to procure sheep's milk and cow's milk from local dairies. The cheese is made on the premises and sold at their own store, and other local retail stores when supply is available.

WHAT MAKES THIS CHEESE SPECIAL?

The Faillace family—Larry, Linda, and their three children (the three shepherds)—started making cheese and were promptly shut down when federal regulations forced their flock to be removed from the farm and destroyed. Their mission for the farm includes supporting local food and community gardening, and their cheesemaking has evolved into only a small part of their overall operation. Local milk is delivered to the farm several days a week, from May until late September, transformed into a raw-milk cheese, and aged in the family's affinage cave, half buried in the earth and having walls filled with straw-bale insulation.

ABOUT THE FARM

LOCATED IN THE SOUTHEAST CORNER of Washington County, on the northernmost tip of the Green Mountain National Forest, is the Mad River Valley and the quintessential New England village of Warren. A charming, classic small town, built around a waterfall, a general store, and the legendary Pitcher Inn, Warren is just two miles away from Three Shepherds of the Mad River Valley farm. The farm is part of ninety-two acres owned by Anne Browning, and, making the most of one of the few flat stretches of land in the area, it is divided into community gardens, an organic flower and vegetable farm, and the cheesemaking building used for cheese by Three Shepherds. The Faillaces have converted an old schoolhouse built in 1897—used as a school until the 1970s, and today still located on the property—into a market to sell their cheese and local produce from neighboring farms.

Since 1998, the Faillace family has been in embroiled in a dispute with the U.S. Department of Agriculture (USDA) over a flock of East Friesian Sheep they imported from the Netherlands in 1996. The flock was traced to a Belgian farm that had animals with bovine

An 1897 schoolhouse has been converted into a store that sells Three Shepherds of the Mad River Valley cheese and other Vermont-made products.

spongiform encephalopathy (BSE, or Mad Cow Disease). In 2001, federal officials removed 125 sheep from the Faillances' farm, suspecting that they were a hazard, and destroyed them; they also required the Faillaces to refrain from having sheep on the land for another five years. Despite ongoing disputes with the USDA, the Faillace family continues to make cheese with sheep and cow milk from neighboring farms. In addition to making cheese, they offer cheese-making classes in a hoop-style greenhouse that serves as a cheese room during the summer. Covered with a double layer of plastic sheeting and shade cloth to protect it from the heat of summer sun, it is a low-maintenance, energy-efficient facility. Finished cheese is aged in a straw-bale cave, buried halfway into the ground to optimize the earth's natural thermal qualities.

2. NEIGHBORLY FARMS OF VERMONT

LINDA AND ROBERT DIMMICK

1362 Curtis Road

Randolph Center, VT 05061

(888) 212-6898

www.neighborlyfarms.com

TYPE OF CHEESE: COW'S MILK

➤ **Raw Milk Cheddar:** This creamy-textured cheddar is made from a classic recipe and in true farmstead fashion— from fresh milk pumped directly from the barn.

➤ **Monterey Jack:** Soft, white, and buttery flavored with an acidic tang, this cheese has a firmer texture than cheddar. It is also blended with jalapeño peppers during the cheesemaking process for Jalapeño Jack.

➤ **Feta:** This feta is made from raw milk, vacuum packed, and aged for sixty days.

➤ **Colby:** Soft with a lacey texture, this high-moisture cheese is the mild version of the company's cheddar.

ABOUT THE CHEESE

While the classic cheddar recipe is the same one used by both Shelburne Farms and Grafton Village Cheese Company, the different type of cow, the different flora on which the cows graze, and, of course, a different process give this cheese a character all its own. Instead of Brown Swiss (Shelburne Farms) or Jersey (Grafton Village Cheese Company), Neighborly Farms has Holsteins, which are known for being hearty milk producers. The cheese is one of the few certified-organic cheeses in the state, and the farm promotes itself as a family destination, where visitors can watch the cheesemaking process and meet the cows. Co-owner Linda Dimmick taught herself to make cheese in her farmhouse kitchen then consulted Vermont cheesemaker Peter Dixon, who helped match the best recipes to the Dimmicks' herd. They chose four easy recipes that require plenty of work up front, yet are sealed in plastic for minimum effort in the affinage process.

WHAT MAKES THIS CHEESE SPECIAL?
At this family farm, located in the heart of central Vermont's dairy country, it was all about saving the cows. While much of the Randolph area south of Interstate 89 has been urbanized, there are still a large number of dairy farmers grazing their animals and selling milk to dairy co-ops, at the mercy of the low market prices. Only five years after Linda and Robert Dimmick converted their dairy, from supplying milk to a local cooperative, to making cheese instead, they met their goal of producing 2,000 pounds a week. The certified-organic cheddar cheese is in high demand at more than 200 health-food stores across the United States.

HOW TO VISIT
Neighborly Farms welcomes visitors from 9 A.M. to 5 P.M., Monday through Saturday. Cheesemaking days are Monday, Wednesday, and Friday. Free cheese samples are available in the store.

DIRECTIONS
From Interstate 89, take exit 4 to Randolph. Go 0.5 mile east on Route 66 to Vermont Technical College. Continue on Route 66 another 0.5 mile and, at the Y intersection, take a left onto Ridge Road. Go 1.4 miles and turn right onto North Randolph Road. Go exactly 1.5 miles to the four corners. Neighborly Farms' big red barn is on the left.

ABOUT THE FARM

IN 1990, LINDA AND ROBERT DIMMICK bought their farm from Robert's parents, who had been farming since the 1960s, but had sold their cows in the mid-1980s. The younger Dimmicks purchased 150 Holsteins and started milking, selling the milk to local dairy co-ops, like their parents had. But by 1993, they were going bankrupt and sold the herd to pay off their bills.

Keeping the land, they continued to make hay on 165 acres to sell to other farmers. In

1998, they decided to give dairy farming another try. This time, they reduced the herd to a mix of forty-eight Holsteins and Jerseys, raising them to meet the stringent certified-organic standards. But instead of selling milk to a dairy co-op like they had before, they were going to make cheese. It was a plan that required them to set up new systems of recording data about their herd and their land, and to develop a cheese to match their milk.

Shortly after implementing organic standards, they noticed a positive change in the health of the herd and began to save enough money in vet bills and fertilizer to show profits. In 2001, cheesemaking began full time, and Neighborly Farms became the first certified-organic cheesemaker in the state. Linda and Robert built a customer-friendly store and viewing room with windows into the cheese room and barn, where visitors can see the whole farmstead-style cheesemaking process, from milking the cows to how the milk is turned into cheese.

Co-owner Linda Dimmick welcomes visitors to Neighborly Farms of Vermont.

The family of five lives in a modest farmhouse across the road from the barn, and every day Linda and Robert walk to work. They have three full-time and four part-time employees who help with the farm chores and cheesemaking. Visitors are allowed to wander into barn, or take pictures of the cows grazing in the fields with a backdrop of picturesque mountains in the distance.

3. BLYTHEDALE FARM

TOM AND BECKY LOFTUS

1471 Cookeville Road

Corinth, VT 05039

(802) 439-6575

TYPE OF CHEESE: COW'S MILK

➤ **Brie** and **Camembert:** These distinctive pasteurized cheeses are left in the aging room just long enough to form a gentle white mold, which ripens the cheese from the outside in, and a natural rind that protects the soft interior. They have delicately assertive flavors and butter-colored, creamy soft fillings. Best if left to ripen at room temperature for a few hours before serving.

➤ **Green Mountain Gruyère:** Made in the traditional Swiss style, this raw-milk, natural-rind cheese has a nutty, buttery flavor and a firm interior. It is ideal for cooking, since it melts uniformly.

➤ **Cookeville Grana:** Aged like an Italian-style Parmesan, this raw-milk cheese has a firm, deep yellow texture and floral, grassy flavor tones. It makes an excellent cheese for grating.

➤ **Jersey Blue:** This cheese is made in the style of Stilton, yet made from whole, unpasteurized milk which makes a dense, creamy curd with a full flavor that is further enhanced by a Roquefort mold.

ABOUT THE CHEESE

Blythedale Farm produces five types of cheese from the 1,300 pounds of rich Jersey milk produced on the farm each day. The cheese can be enjoyed while young and fresh, or it can sit at room temperature under a cheese dome, for a stronger, ripened product. Soft-ripened cheeses are considered the most difficult of cheeses to make because they require a lot of hands-on care. Blythedale Farm uses only lightly pasteurized whole milk and hand-ladles all the cheeses, which are naturally drained and aged for several weeks before distribution to retail stores and restaurants.

WHAT MAKES THIS CHEESE SPECIAL?

Blythedale Farm Camembert and Brie cheese is a time-sensitive product that is labor intensive to make and tricky to age. Becky is largely responsible for making the cheese, and she does so four days a week with the help of local cheesemaker Bessie Sandberg, who has been making cheese at the farm for several years.

The high-butterfat milk of Jersey cows is ideal for the farm's line of rich cheese products. The milk is pumped uphill from the barn to the milking room tank, where it is slowly pasteurized and cultures are added—a process that takes all day. Once the fresh cheese has been formed into small rounds and left to drain, it is transferred to shelves in the curing room for several weeks before being wrapped and shipped to retail stores. The Cookville Grana and Jersey Blue, the two raw-milk aged cheeses, are left in the aging caves for several months to fully develop their natural rind, buttery interior, and mellow flavor.

HOW TO VISIT

Tom and Becky Loftus work around the clock, and while they would love to have visitors, they simply don't have time. However, you can call ahead to arrange special visits and to view the cheesemaking from a window off the shipping area in the cheese room.

DIRECTIONS

Take Route 302 East and turn off onto Route 25 East, toward Bradford. Take a right turn onto Brook Road at Monty's garage/service station. Go right at the fork in the road onto Cookeville Road. Enter the town of Corinth, and Blythedale Farm is on the left, behind the old town hall.

ABOUT THE FARM

IN 1880, THERE WERE 30,000 SHEEP and 1,900 people nestled into the hilly thirty-six-square-mile pocket of Vermont known as Corinth. Founded in the 1760s around a farming culture, today's Corinth is made up of several small towns with a population of about 1,200 and a few dairy and sheep farms still scattered throughout. Blythedale Farm's steep hill is testament to the difficult farming conditions that prevail

Naturally aging Grana and Green Mountain Gruyère cheese in the caves at Blythedale Farm.

in this area. The farm was once known as the David Hastings Farm. Hastings's family built the farmhouse and the large, three-story barn. Hastings kept milking cows in the barn until 1974, then housed draft horses there until 1994, when the farm was sold. The new owners started making Blythedale Farm cheese.

In August 2004, Tom and Becky Loftus purchased Blythedale Farm, which came with a nineteenth-century barn, a newer barn and cheese room, forty acres, and a herd of fifty Jersey cows. The cheese room, equipment, and recipes for continuing the Blythedale Farm soft-ripened cheese were part of the deal, and the Loftuses haven't missed a step. In fact, they have doubled production since they arrived, also upgrading the milking equipment and cheese house. They continue to craft outstanding cheese in the Vermont tradition.

Hobby cheesemakers for ten years, Becky and Tom farmed a small herd in Scottsville, New York, before moving to Vermont, bringing with them their experience and in-depth knowledge of the craft.

They harvest all their own hay, baling and storing it in the old barn and making cheese four days a week throughout the year. Well tended by devoted caretakers, the herd resides in a clean, dry barn and eats no fermented hay. Taking exceptional care of their animals helps Tom and Becky produce exceptional cheeses. And their cheese—and their hard work—is keeping this historic Vermont dairy farm alive.

Tom and Becky Loftus, owners of Blythdale Farm, with one of their Jersey cows.

4. VERMONT BUTTER & CHEESE COMPANY

ALLISON HOOPER AND BOB REESE

P.O. Box 95

40 Pitman Road

Websterville, VT 05678

(802) 479-9371

www.vtbutterandcheeseco.com

TYPE OF CHEESE: GOAT'S MILK

➤ **Fresh Vermont Chèvre:** This chèvre has a mild, fresh flavor and a creamy, spreadable texture. It is available plain or rolled in pepper or herbs.

➤ **Creamy Goat Cheese:** This smooth and spreadable cheese is flavored with imported olives and *herbes de Provence* or roasted red peppers.

➤ **Goat Feta:** Made in the traditional Greek style, this feta's mild, fresh flavor is enhanced by a lower-salt brine.

➤ **Bijou:** With its mild balance of sweet and sour, this soft, aged cheese is wonderful served warm on a baguette with a salad.

➤ **Bonne Bouche:** The name is French for "tasty little bite." This ash-ripened, aged, artisanal cheese is made by hand in the traditional French style. It is sweet and gentle in flavor and has a very creamy texture.

➤ **Coupole:** Hand-shaped into a dome, this mild, dense, delicate cheese is lightly salted, and sprinkled with french vegetable ash known as cendre, imported from France during aging. The slightly creamy center has a lively flavor whether eaten fresh or allowed to ripen over time.

ABOUT THE CHEESE

The French once cornered the market on chèvre, yet Vermont Butter & Cheese Company's chèvre is every bit as delicious as imported cheese. Because you can't have too much of good thing, the chèvre comes in four variations—plain, herb, pepper, and a combination—and is available in three sizes. The milk for all the cheese products is pasteurized before it is made into cheese. Once the curd has drained, it is lifted into a hopper and formed into logs, which are hand-rolled in herbs and vacuum sealed to remain fresh for shipping. In addition to its fresh cheese, the company has recently introduced three new aged goat cheeses based on traditional French recipes.

WHAT MAKES THIS CHEESE SPECIAL?

Consistency and *control* are the key words when producing a quality product at the level that Vermont Butter & Cheese Company does. The company ships its products all over the United States.

Five years in development, the aged goat cheeses are a step up from the fresh cheeses. The aged cheeses are not "farmers' market" cheese, but rather a high-end product for discriminating chefs. French cheesemaker Adeline Folley has been added to the staff, and a new facility has been built exclusively for this aged cheese. The cheese is prepared, drained, salted, and sprinkled with ash, then left to develop for twelve days in three separate, highly monitored temperature- and humidity-controlled rooms. Everything in the building is meticulously washed to ensure the environment is optimal for the positive microflora to perform the proper affinage on the cheese. Once ripened, the rounds of cheese are placed in custom-made wooden crates and wrapped with plastic; the plastic contains air holes that allow the cheese to continue to ripen during storage and shipping. The result is an outstanding sweet-and-sour flavor and a creamy texture that matches the best French chèvres.

HOW TO VISIT

Located in the Wilson Industrial Park, the company has recently added a viewing gallery for visitors to watch cheesemaking, read about the process, and buy cheese.

DIRECTIONS

Take Interstate 89 to exit 6. Go to bottom of the hill and straight through the intersection with Route 14, but do not turn onto Route 14. At the top of the hill, turn left on Graniteville Road. Take the first right onto Websterville Road and left onto Pitman Road. Wilson Industrial Park is on the left. Vermont Butter & Cheese Company is the green building.

ABOUT THE COMPANY

WHEN VERMONT BUTTER & CHEESE COMPANY was launched in 1984, nobody was even having a conversation about American cheese, let alone goat cheese. Fresh out of college, Allison Hooper learned to make goat cheese on a farm in France. Later, after returning to the United States, she launched the Vermont Butter & Cheese Company with business partner Bob Reese, the former marketing director at the Vermont Department of Agriculture. They started with a single product: chèvre. They were among the first chèvre cheesemakers in the United States, and one of the first artisan cheesemakers in Vermont. Their focus has always been on producing a high-quality product and partnering with farmers who produce high-quality milk.

Good things—in this case, Vermont Butter & Cheese Company's French-style Bonne Bouche cheese—come in small packages.

In the beginning, Allison would drive her pick-up truck to the farms to collect the goats' milk in ten-gallon stainless-steel cans. As the business grew, the farmers began to deliver directly to the cheesemaking facility, pouring the milk into a storage tank that would be piped into the cheese room. Recognizing that driving to the factory took time away from the farm, Allison and Bob contracted with a local milk hauler, Pouliot & Corriveau of Williamstown, to collect and deliver the milk. As of 2006, 3,000 gallons of goat's milk from seventeen farms around Vermont is delivered twice a week. Over the years, Vermont Butter & Cheese has added a variety of products beyond chèvre, including crème fraiche, fromage blanc, mascarpone, and cultured butter—all of which incorporate cow's milk bought from the St. Albans Cooperative. All the milk is rBGH (recombinant bovine growth hormone) free.

Allison and Bob stay connected to the farmers that supply milk, recognizing their role in the success of the business, and make every effort to keep them profitable and sustainable. Allison is currently writing a manual about goat farming in the hopes that cow dairy farmers who are thinking about leaving that industry will consider switching over to milking goats. The cheesemaking facility is pristine and state of the art. French-trained cheesemaker Adeline Folley joined the company in 2003 to oversee the production, quality, research, and design of cheese. While the business has grown considerably in the past twenty-two years, with thirty-one employees, and more cheesemakers are offering goats' milk products, Vermont Butter & Cheese Company remains one of the top goat's milk cheesemakers in the country.

Vermont Butter & Cheese Company's domed Coupole cheese is shaped in molds. Photo courtesy of Vermont Butter & Cheese Company.

5. CABOT CREAMERY COOPERATIVE

Main Street

Cabot, VT 05647

(800) 837-4261

www.cabotcheese.coop

TYPE OF CHEESE: COW'S MILK

➤ **Mild Cheddar:** This cheddar is aged for two to three months to produce a creamy flavor and smooth consistency.

➤ **Sharp Aged Cheddar:** This cheddar is aged for at least five to eight months and has a silky, well-developed flavor.

➤ **Extra Aged Cheddar:** The rich flavor and dense texture is the result of aging for nine to fourteen months.

➤ **Seriously Sharp Cheddar:** Its flavor varies from vat to vat but always provides that old-fashioned cheddar bite; this cheddar is aged for ten months.

➤ **Private Stock Cheddar:** Aged for one and a half years, this sharp cheddar is the favorite among the professional graders at Cabot for its clean cheddar taste and creamy textures. It is sharp without any bitter qualities and is considered the perfect cheddar flavor.

➤ **Vintage Cheddar:** Originally known as President's Choice, this aged cheese has Cabot's president/big cheese Rich Stammer's name on every hand-dipped bar. It is aged at least two years before it is ready for market. The dry texture has an intense flavor that lingers.

ABOUT THE CHEESE

With over two dozen different cheddar types to choose from, Cabot is the state's largest cheese producer and the largest producer of dairy products in general, although it is still small by national standards. Cabot cheddar brings home many awards and high accolades from a variety of domestic and international cheese competitions. Its clothbound cheddar won "Best Cheddar" at the 1998 and 2006 World Championship Cheese Contests and "Best in Show" at the 2006 American

Cheese Society Awards. All of Cabot's cheddars are made naturally, without chemicals or preservatives, wrapped in plastic, and aged for specific flavor profiles in a nearby facility.

Cabot Creamery, one of the founding members of the Vermont Cheese Council, is now collaborating with the Kehler brothers at Jasper Hill Farm in Greensboro to produce a natural-rind, cheesecloth-bound cheddar. These thirty-eight-pound wheels expel moisture and after ten months of aging in a cellar, end up at thirty-four pounds each. In 2006, less than 12,000 pounds of Cabot clothbound cheddar was aged, yet due to their 2006 Best of Show award at the American Cheese Society annual event, plans are afoot to expand the aging cellar at Jasper Hill, to increase that capacity twentyfold in the coming years.

WHAT MAKES THIS CHEESE SPECIAL?

Pride is the key word to describe this farmers' cooperative and its dedication to manufacturing the very best products from the highest-quality milk. Cabot's three professional graders—Earle, Oscar, and Ted—have sixty-five years of combined experience and taste every batch. Their trained taste buds determine if a batch is deemed mild, sharp, or extra-sharp category as much as the calendar does.

HOW TO VISIT

Cabot Creamery receives over 100,000 visitors each year at its three visitors' center–retail stores, located in Cabot, on Route 100 in Waterbury Center, and on Route 4 near the Quechee Gorge.

The visitors' center in Cabot is open every day, June to October from 9 A.M. to 5 P.M., and factory tours are available every half hour. The tour includes a ten-minute video on cheesemaking and the history of Cabot, plus a fifteen-minute guided walk through the main production area.

From November to May, the store closes at 4 P.M. and is closed all day on Sunday.

DIRECTIONS

From Interstate 89, take exit 8 at Montpelier. Take Route 2 east to Marshfield, and go left on Route 215. Follow Route 215 five miles to the village of Cabot.

ABOUT THE COMPANY

THE VILLAGE OF CABOT is an old-fashioned Vermont town with the basic necessities, such as a hardware store, general store, and town office lining the Main Street, and simple farmhouses with wide porches flanking either side. Around the Fourth of July, American flags flank the street as residents celebrate with their customary annual parade. Just past Main Street, across from the firehouse, the creamery's white metal milk tanks, decorated with the Cabot logo, rise above the treeline in the site of Cabot's original creamery, in continuous operation since 1893.

Cabot is home to Vermont's most historic dairy co-op, which began in 1919 with ninety-five local dairy farmers. Each contributed five dollars per cow to buy the local creamery, which shipped milk to Boston via train. Today, 1,400 throughout New England farmers belong to the Cabot family of cooperative farmers, and Cabot provides incentive premiums for their high-quality milk. Operating profits are split among the farmers at the end of the year based on the quantity and quality of milk each provides. Over the years, Cabot Creamery has grown by acquiring other milk cooperatives, and in 1992 it merged with Agri-Mark, the leading dairy cooperative in the Northeast. Today Cabot gathers milk from over one-quarter of Vermont's nearly 1,200 dairy farms for their cheese and other products.

On the tour at the creamery, visitors can watch as the milk is heated to 165 degrees to pasteurize it, then cooled to 85 degrees. The milk is pumped into four large cooking vats, each able to hold about 5,000 gallons of milk, which will ultimately yield roughly 4,000 pounds of cheese. Cheese starter cultures are added to the milk, and then rennet is added to coagulate the milk or "set the vat." About two hours later, after the custardlike "set" has been cut and gently cooked at upwards of 100 degrees, the curds and whey are transferred to one of three finishing tables in the warm (85-degree) cheese room. Rotating rakes stir the curd as the whey is drained off the finishing table. The curd, after being salted by hand, is then shoveled and pushed into an auger with a wide-mouthed hose. It is transferred to the top of two high towers where the weight of the curds and vacuum pressure combine to knit the curd into thirty-eight-pound blocks. These blocks are immediately sealed in airtight plastic and shipped to an aging room, where millions of pounds of cheese rotate through storage, aging all the way.

While not exactly farmstead produced, Cabot cheese is arguably the most renowned Vermont cheese in the world. Though the cheesemaking operation is on a grand scale, visiting the creamery is a good way to see the process and appreciate the work, history, and contributions of the many cooperative dairy farmers of the region.

The visitors' center at Cabot Creamery, the largest cheese producer and the largest producer of dairy products in the state.

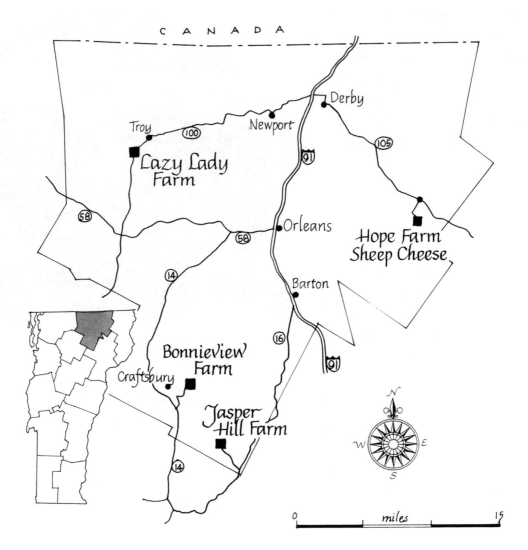

CANADA

Derby

Troy

Newport

100

105

91

Lazy Lady
Farm

58

58

Orleans

Hope Farm
Sheep Cheese

14

Barton

16

91

Bonnieview
Farm

Craftsbury

Jasper
Hill Farm

14

N

W   E

S

0   miles   15

140

CHAPTER 6

ESSEX AND ORLEANS COUNTIES

Greensboro • Craftsbury Common • Westfield • East Charleston

HE NORTHEAST KINGDOM COVERS THREE COUNTIES, and is bordered by Canada and New Hampshire on two sides. This region is wild and rural, sparsely populated, and undeveloped in comparison to some of the other parts of Vermont. The major highway, Interstate 91, runs through the center of Caledonia County, and more roads travel north and south than east to west. Spectacular lakes dot the valleys throughout this region, and stretches of open hayfields are balanced by dramatic mountain backdrops. It is easy to see why Caspian Lake in Greensboro and Lake Willoughby in Westmore attract summer visitors. The quiet country villages offer respite; many village centers consist of a single country store, and neighbors are separated by miles of hayfields.

In spite of the area's rural nature, there are four excellent cheesemakers in this region, with a range of goat, sheep, and cow herds. All of these local cheesemakers started on a small scale, selling their cheese at the local farmers' markets. Word of these companies' award-winning cheese has spread beyond Vermont, and the UPS driver is seen as often as the Agri-Mark dairy cooperative truck on the rural back roads. The familiar brown van ambles down the dirt road, passing tractors and other farm vehicles, to pick up carefully insulated packages of fresh cheese that will be delivered the next day to stores and restaurants across the country.

Greensboro, located on Capsian Lake, is mostly a summer resort, and it is a bonus that **Jasper Hill Farm** (1) is only a few miles outside of town. Drive down a steep driveway to an old barnyard, and you'll find a newly built cheesemaking facility with state-of-the-art equipment and a hidden cave beneath, for affinage of their own cheese as well as that of other Vermont cheesemakers. Magnificent views of distant fields and mountains were only part of the reason the Kehler brothers bought the farm. To preserve a way of life that they saw rapidly disappearing and to keep the farmland open and alive, they contracted a business plan that was based on making world-class cheese. A few miles north, in Craftsbury Common, Neil Urie of **Bonnieview Farm** (2) follows in the footsteps of several generations of dairy farmers who made a living on his family farm. When his turn came, he chose to raise sheep instead of cows. His large flock produces enough milk for his own brand of cheese, as well as for other area cheesemakers.

Lazy Lady Farm (3) is off the beaten path and off the grid, and that's just the way Laini Fondiller wants to remain. Laini learned to make cheese while traveling in France as a farmhand, came back to Vermont and began to produce a handcrafted product that is aged in a custom-built underground cave, regulated by geothermal temperatures.

The final farm on this chapter's tour is **Hope Farm Sheep Cheese** (4), located in a low-lying valley. Though this farm looks the same as the other dairy farms along this rural dirt road, owners Barbara and Harvey Levin raise a flock of sheep instead of a herd of Holsteins. Leaving their professional lives for a quiet life on the farm, the Levins started making cheese to support their love for sheep, and the rest, as they say, is history.

1. JASPER HILL FARM

MATEO AND ANDY KEHLER

884 Garvin Hill Road

Greensboro, VT 05841

(802) 533-2566

www.jasperhillfarm.com

TYPE OF CHEESE: COW'S MILK

➤ **Aspenhurst:** A variation of traditional English Leicester Cheddar, it is hand-made, cloth-bound cheese with a full-bodied elegance. Created exclusively from the milk or the farm's Ayrshire cows and aged for a minimum of twelve months.

➤ **Bayley Hazen Blue:** With its natural rind and blue veining, this raw-milk cheese is exceptionally creamy and smooth, yet the texture is drier and more crumbly than most blues. The taste is reminiscent of chocolate and butter, and each wheel is carefully aged from four and six months.

➤ **Constant Bliss:** This soft, mold-ripened, high-moisture, raw-milk cheese is formed into a distinctive pyramid shape. Natural microflora in the milk, which change with the seasons, result in variations on the surface and in the flavor of the cheese. Careful affinage is the key to the success of this highly regarded cheese.

ABOUT THE CHEESE

Cheesemaking is a family affair at Jasper Hill Farm. To ensure that he's using milk that is as fresh as can be, Mateo Kehler begins the cheesemaking process before his brother, Andy, even finishes milking the Ayrshire herd. Victoria, Andy's wife, is the head affineuse, while Angela, Mateo's wife, is responsible for the production of the Constant Bliss cheese and keeps the books for the rapidly expanding business.

Ayrshire cow's milk is particularly well suited to cheese production because the small fat globules are easily broken down during the aging process. The newly built and modern-equipped cheese room is connected to the milking parlor and barn, and a trap door leads down to the caves beneath. The cheese is aged on ash and pine shelves; the temperature in the cave's chambers is carefully controlled to produce different optimal temperature zones, and the turning of the cheese is monitored to encourage healthy spore development during affinage.

WHAT MAKES THIS CHEESE SPECIAL?
Andy and Mateo understand that cheese will never be any better than the quality of the milk, and their Ayrshire cows receive only the best treatment. Proper affinage is instrumental to the quality and consistency of their products, and the cheese is kept at optimal conditions in a special underground facility.

In the Vermont tradition, their cheese names reflect the history of the area around the farm. Bayley Hazen Blue is named after an old military road that traverses the Northeast Kingdom; the road was commissioned by General George Washington to carry troops to fight the English on a Canadian front. Though no battle ever took place, the road brought Greensboro its first settlers and continues to be used. Aspenhurst is a cellar-matured cheddar named after part of the north shore of Caspian Lake in Greensboro, while Constant Bliss honors a Revolutionary War scout killed in Greensboro in 1781.

HOW TO VISIT
Due to construction during 2007 and the farm's high profile, Jasper Hill Farm is not open to the public until further notice. Their cheese is available in the Willeys Store in the center of Greensboro as well as other locations nationwide.

DIRECTIONS
Available by special invitation only

Jasper Hill Cheese just after pressing, and ready to be transferred to the aging cellar.

ABOUT THE FARM

SMALL AND UPSCALE, with a lively general store and ambience, Greensboro is famous for beautiful Caspian Lake, a favorite summer destination, and Circkus Smirkus, Vermont's one-and-only youth circus. But this small town is also home to Jasper Hill Farm, which is quickly becoming one of Vermont's most well-known and highly regarded artisanal cheese brands.

Though raised in South America, brothers Andy and Mateo Kehler summered in Greensboro as children. In 1993, Andy wandered back to the area and bought 220 acres and an old dairy barn, formerly known as the Jasper Hill Farm. Located just three miles outside of town, the farm has spectacular views, and the open fields are verdant and lush. Over 30 percent of the dairy farms in Greensboro were lost the year he purchased the farm, and with the price of real estate in this area, Andy could have easily turned a profit by building homes for sale. But instead, he decided to go into business with his brother and raise cows to make cheese, thus keeping the landscape open and maintaining its natural beauty.

In 2001, they finalized a business plan that included purchasing fifty Ayrshire cows, known for producing milk with qualities for excellent cheese—blue cheese in particular. Over several years, they learned to raise animals and make

Variations in the natural microflora give each batch of Jasper Hill Farm's Constant Bliss cheese a unique surface texture and appearance.

145

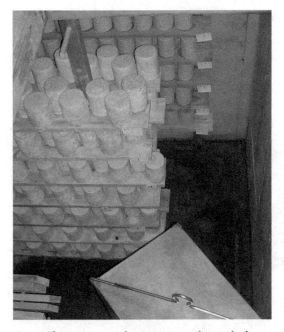

A trap door opens to the aging caves beneath the Jasper Hill Farm cheese room. The cheeses rest on ash and pine shelves.

cheese. Mateo spent two years in London, including six months at Neal's Dairy Yard, to immerse himself in the world of cheese, while Andy added to the herd and set up the barn for milking. Together they designed and built a state-of-the-art cheese room, attached to the barn, and a full-sized cellar equipped with separate chambers to maintain specific temperature-controlled conditions. The cellar holds hundreds of wheels of cheese on its pine and ash boards. Pallets of cheese are lowered into the cellar through a trap door in the cheese-room floor or are carried down the cellar steps.

The Kehlers' long-term goal is to produce cheeses of the highest quality from their own milk and to demonstrate that it is still possible to prosper on a rocky, hillside Vermont farm. But they also hope their business model can be replicated on other Vermont dairy farms, the state's dairy economy can be renewed. To accomplish this goal, in 2007 they will be expanding the cheesemaking cellars at Jasper Hill to have space to naturally age cheese for other cheesemakers through carefully controlled affinage. Smaller farmstead cheesemakers such as Bonnieview Farm already use their cellars for aging, as do larger cheesemakers such as Cabot Creamery and Grafton Village Cheese Company.

2. BONNIEVIEW FARM

Neil Urie
2228 South Albany Road
Craftsbury Common, VT 05827
(802) 755-2566

TYPE OF CHEESE: SHEEP'S MILK

➤ **Ben Nevis:** This distinctive dome-shaped, square cheese, named after the highest mountain in Scotland, develops a bloomy rind that is cultured in the recipe and created by brining in whey for the first few weeks.

➤ **Ewe's Feta:** Left to age for sixty days in containers of brine, this creamy white feta is slightly salted. The results are an excellent texture and flavor—lovely, blended into a green salad. It is a favorite with local customers.

➤ **Mossend Blue:** This creamy blue cheese with a natural rind is aged seventy to a hundred days in the cellar.

flock and makes cheese only during the six months that his sheep are lactating, from May to October. This limited schedule guarantees that the cheese is as fresh as the lush fields of clover and timothy that surround the farm.

Three days a week, Neil produces an average of thirty seven-pound wheels of his special aged blue cheese, Mossend Blue, named after his ancestral home in Scotland. The more popular square-shaped cheese called Ben Nevis takes two days to make. The curds are hand-pressed to release the whey, then the cheese is allowed to air dry before it is transferred to the caves at Jasper Hill Farm for affinage.

ABOUT THE CHEESE
Made in small batches by hand, Bonnieview Farm sheep's milk cheese is made on a small family farm. Neil Urie tends the

WHAT MAKES THIS CHEESE SPECIAL?
Committed to saving the family farm, Neil switched from cows to sheep as a way to keep the fields in a healthy crop rotation,

while creating a product that is unique to the area. The flock is carefully managed and resides in the lush fields, within view of the cheese room. The fresh sheep's milk is heated, and once curds are formed, Neil and a helper stir constantly while slicing the curds into small fragments. Transferring the curds into forms, they hand-press each cheese several times to release the whey, which drips into a bucket and is piped into an exterior tank to be fed to the milking ewes.

HOW TO VISIT
Bonnieview is a small family farm and has only one cheesemaker, who also tends the livestock and manages the fields. Visitors are welcome, and school children often make pilgrimages here to feed the young sheep in the spring. A picture window allows visitors to view the small cheese room from the outside.

DIRECTIONS
Take Route 14 to Craftsbury. Continue towards South Craftsbury but after one mile, turn right onto East Craftsbury Road. Take the second left onto South Albany Road (a dirt road) and go three miles. Bonnieview Farm is the third farm on the left.

ABOUT THE FARM

THE THREE-MILE DRIVE down the dirt road to Bonnieview Farm is one of the most bucolic in the state. Pastoral views either side, a ridgeline of mountains rises in the distance, and arching trees form green tunnels. It's easy to see why Neil Urie is determined to maintain the farm, where five generations of family members preceded him. Neil shares his story of how four Scottish settlers came to the valley in 1829 and then beckoned other Scottish farmers to join them. By 1890, dozens of dairy farms lined the road, bringing milk to a local creamery and butter to Boston by train.

After graduating from engineering school in 1990 and spending two years in the Peace Corps, helping Jamaican farmers establish local livestock practices, Neil bought the family farm from his great-uncle in September, 1993. The estate included 470 acres, 207 acres of which was pure open pasture; an old farmhouse; several large barns; and seventy-five Holstein cows. Frustrated by the low price of milk, he sold the herd and visited the Majors at Vermont Shepherd in Putney to learn to make cheese. In 1997, he bought sixty East Friesian sheep and brought them to Bonnieview Farm.

For a number of years, all the cheese made at Bonnieview Farm was sent to Vermont Shepherd. Once a week, Neil packed 400 pounds of cheese into a jeep and drove it to the aging caves in Putney. Once aged, it was then sold as Vermont Shepherd cheese. Now he makes his own brand of handmade cheese, cultivating three distinctive raw-milk recipes and hand-pressing the curds in a cheese room built solely for this purpose.

Neil Urie pours curds into cylindrical molds in the cheese room at Bonnieview Farm.

The cheese room is located across the road from the farmhouse and the barn, requiring him to transfer the milk a short distance to the cheese vats. A free-standing cooler acts as an aging room, but this cooler it is not nearly large enough to hold all the cheese. To meet the increased demand for Bonnieview Farm cheese, some wheels are now carefully transferred to the cellars at Jasper Hill, where they are rotated and aged on ash boards to create a natural-rind cheese with character.

3. LAZY LADY FARM

LAINI FONDILLER

973 Snyderbrook Road

Westfield, VT 05874

(802) 744-6365

TYPE OF CHEESE: GOAT'S MILK, COW'S MILK

➤ **Les Pyramids:** This pasteurized goat cheese has the flavor of a dense, robust, classic chèvre.

➤ **Demi-Tasse:** This mixed-milk Camembert-Brie hybrid is aged two to four weeks.

➤ **Trillium:** A sweet, smooth, pasteurized goat's milk chèvre and a buttery cow cheese are layered with vegetable ash imported from France to create this delicate combination cheese.

➤ **Valencay:** A true French classic, this pasteurized, semisoft goat cheese has an ash coating and a rich goaty and salty flavor.

➤ **Marbarella:** Layered with ash, this pasteurized goat cheese is sweet, smooth, and velvety. The flavors are most pro-

nounced when it is with served with sourdough bread.

➤ **Capriola:** This pasteurized goat cheese has the intensely buttery qualities typical of French chèvre.

➤ **La Roche:** This nicely salted pasteurized goat cheese has dense texture and a tangy afterbite.

➤ **Tomme DeLay:** To make this raw-milk goat cheese, lightly heated curd is aged with a hint of summer savory and thyme to produce a delicate, sweet flavor.

➤ **Buck Hill Sunshine:** The company describes this pasteurized cow's milk cheese as "whey better than Brie," but with the same soft-ripened qualities.

➤ **Fil-a-Buster:** This raw cow's milk cheese has a creamy washed rind and a firm, yet moist, texture.

ABOUT THE CHEESE

Lazy Lady Farm won its first blue ribbon at the 1999 American Cheese Society awards for its Les Pyramids cheese. With this recognition, owner and cheesemaker Laini Fondiller switched from selling solely at the local farmers' markets to shipping cheese off premises. All her recipes are classic French-style chèvres, and their names reflect their French heritage. Most of the cheeses are made with goat's milk that is lightly pasteurized; all have a natural rind and are aged for a minimum of sixty days in an underground cave. The cheese is carefully ripened to encourage a gentle mold to grow on the exterior, and it is packaged in a way that allows the cheese to ripen naturally from the inside out.

WHAT MAKES THIS CHEESE SPECIAL?

Lazy Lady cheese is very French in quality and flavor. The dense, buttery, rich, creamy chèvre has a strong bite and tangy aftertaste, just the way the French like their cheese. The soft-ripened qualities are also characteristic of French chèvre. Laini explains that she learned to make cheese this way in Corsica and adapted the recipe to the geography of Westfield, Vermont, and the seasonal nature of the milk produced by her goats.

Laini and her partner, Barry Shaw, love their goats and always treat the animals with respect, taking extra care in the barn to maintain a level of cleanliness that is optimal for the goat's health and gives the animals a stress-free environment. The flock is the heart of the business; the goats graze and grow in ideal conditions—pastures kept lush with wild flowers, herbs, and grasses. Their cheese is certified organic by the Northeast Organic Farming Association of Vermont (NOFA-VT) regulation standards.

HOW TO VISIT

Lazy Lady Farm is not set up to receive visitors, although you can call ahead to arrange up a visit and get directions. From May through October, Laini can be found at the Montpelier farmers' market and occasionally offers cheesemaking classes in the winter months at her farm.

DIRECTIONS

Provided by prior arrangement only

ABOUT THE FARM

*L*AZY LADY FARM is off the grid, powered only by solar cells and a wind tower. Laini and Barry hand-built their house and post-and-beam barn, as well as the cheese room and cave for their handmade goat's milk cheese. Located down a winding path from the house, the aging cave, with its arched doorway, is like a secret hobbit house. Two doors form an air lock; one closes before the other is opened, to keep the temperature inside and the air in synch with the natural geothermal heat of the earth.

Laini grew up in Indiana, graduated from college with a teaching degree, and immediately fell into a farming life, starting with a hog farm, then worked with cows, sheep, and goats. For a decade she worked on farms all around New England and France, knocking on farmers' doors and offering to work. She asked for nothing in return but the experience, room, and board. In 1986, back in Vermont, she worked at Butterworks Farm, met Barry Shaw, a carpenter, and together they settled on thirty-five acres in rural Vermont.

Contrary to what the farm's name implies, Laini is anything but a lazy lady. The first summer on the farm, she planted a large garden to grow vegetables to sell at the farmers' market and bought seven ewes and one goat for milking. She made cheese in her kitchen, using recipes and techniques from her farm experience in France. The cheese ripened on shelves in a storage closet that had been lined with plastic to catch the dripping whey. But the cheese did not taste or behave like the cheese in France, and it took Laini a while to figure out why the French recipes did not work with the same recipes, for cheese made in Vermont. Long before others in Vermont were making farmstead goat cheese, she had to figure it out on her own, and she did. The final cheese was an instant hit.

The weathered gray barn at Lazy Lady Farm provides shelter for the goats.

She reduced her vegetable growing business and planted one-third of an acre to garlic, a crop that requires less attention. During the winter, when the goats were dry, Laini cleaned out the milk room, set up her loom, and wove and made felt and rugs from her sheep's wool. In the summer, Laini sold cheese and garlic, along with her handmade, hand-loomed rugs, at the farmers' market.

Goats and cheesemaking grew into an integral part the farm, and by 1990, Barry had built a new barn. In 1996, he constructed a new cheese room for making the goat cheese, which would be ripened in the underground aging cave. By the summer of 2002, Laini was milking twenty goats and turning twenty gallons of milk per day into four batches of eight different types of cheese, seven days a week.

Currently, Laini and Barry raise thirty-three registered certified-organic Alpine goats, selected from top breeding stock. The Alpine breed combines the best milk production with show-quality looks. Laini makes cheese

Laini Fondiller, owner of Lazy Lady Farm, stands by the entrance to her custom-built cheese-aging cave.

five days a week, and she has recently added some cow's milk cheeses to her product line, bringing the total amount of cheese produced to 8,000 pounds per year. She continues to make the cheese, while Barry tends the goats, and a part-time helper assists with affinage, wrapping, and shipping the cheese to distributors and stores.

Twenty years after they started, their lives are still busy and far from lazy, but Laini and Barry take great pride in their handmade lifestyle, their farm, and their cheeses. Laini describes herself as having the curiosity of a cat, and each season offers a range of new twists on classic recipes to enhance her line of already extraordinary chèvre.

4. HOPE FARM SHEEP CHEESE

BARBARA AND HARVEY LEVIN

P.O. Box 164

1984 Hudson Road

East Charleston, VT 05833

(802) 723-4283

TYPE OF CHEESE: SHEEP'S MILK

➤ **Tomme de Brébis:** Made from raw milk, this farmstead cheese is firm and smooth with mild, buttery overtones. It has an edible, soft gold rind with an overlay of white mold, Made from high-quality sheep's milk, it is ready at two months and continues to develop to five months of age.

➤ **Pierce Hill:** Based on a washed-curd Gouda recipe, this cheese has a natural rind that is washed with balsamic vinegar. Aged for a minimum of three months, this moist, firm-textured cheese has a sweet, nutty finish typical of Gouda, and a full flavor from the high butterfat of the sheep's milk.

➤ **Summer Daze:** This popular feta cheese is aged sixty days in brine before being cut into wedges for sale. Firm, with a dry texture, it is less salty than other feta. It is very popular at local farmers' markets during the summer

ABOUT THE CHEESE

Hope Farm currently has about forty Lacaune/Freisian sheep. Barbara and Harvey Levin make cheese every other day from mid-May through October and produce three distinctly different aged, raw sheep's milk cheeses, including a natural-rind tomme, a feta, and a Gouda-like cheese. Since this is a raw-milk, aged cheese, production starts in May (after lambing), but the cheese is not available for sale until August. The Levins are both involved in the whole process, from milking through the final months of aging, and the cheese has the superior quality of a carefully handmade and monitored product.

WHAT MAKES THIS CHEESE SPECIAL?
What began as a hobby has escalated into a seasonal full-time business, and demand for Hope Farm sheep cheese outweighs the supply. The Levins have one of the smallest commercial cheesemaking operations in the state, producing just 2,000 pounds of raw-milk sheep cheese in 2006–2007. They are meticulous about their sheep and their cheese, with most of their sales taking place at the local farmers' market, where Barbara also sells wool and frozen lamb meat. They made their first cheese in the fall of 2002, after working through several recipes and finally settling on one that met their standards. They continue to streamline operations and hope to increase production, but not by a lot, just enough for two people to handle.

HOW TO VISIT
Visitors are welcome as time permits. Please call ahead.

DIRECTIONS
Enter West Charleston on Route 105 and go another five miles to the junction at the East Charleston country store. Turn right onto Twin Bridges Road, and go one mile to an intersection with Hudson Road. Go right onto Hudson Road, and the sheep will be on your right. The farm has no sign; look for the farmhouse with natural cedar siding and green trim and for the sheet-metal-domed barn directly on the road.

ABOUT THE FARM

WHEN BARBARA AND HARVEY LEVIN moved to Hope Farm in 2001, passing neighbors slowed down to stare at their small flock of fifteen sheep. Few had seen sheep in this mostly Holstein dairy region of Vermont, and the Levins' farm was the first to convert into a sheep farm.

While many pockets of the Northeast Kingdom have scenic lake regions that attract summer people seeking vacation homes, others boast affordable farmland for sale. Attracted

Barbara and Harvey Levin with one member of their flock of Lacaune/Freisian sheep

to the notion of plenty of acreage, the Levins bought thirty-seven acres of rich bottomland and a modest, cedar-sided house with a view of cedar woods and neighboring dairy farms. Both were retired from professional occupations; Barbara was a physical therapist, while Harvey was a mechanical engineer. Neither had any experience farming or cheesemaking, other than raising sheep as a hobby. Over the past five years, however, their flock has grown to several dozen milking ewes, and they sell twice that number as meat lambs. They produce three excellent raw-milk cheeses, selling at several farmers' markets and delivering them to chefs and stores. Their cheese inventory is usually sold out by the end of December.

To keep the farm and cheesemaking manageable for two people, Harvey built and rigged the pristine cheese room and milking parlor with labor-saving devices to press the cheese curds and extract the whey. The milk is kept in milk cans immersed in 34-degree water, and transferred into the cheese room for cheesemaking every other day. Ripening takes place in a temperature-controlled room, and each cheese is washed with brine and hand-turned until it is ready for sale.

The Levins still consider themselves retired, although during the five months that they milk the herd and make cheese, they work without any outside help from dawn to dusk. Though Harvey continues to use his engineering know-how to design and build labor-saving devices for their cheese business, Barbara mourns the loss of time for a summer vegetable garden. But this perfect two-person operation supports the farm and allows the Levins to enjoy a rural lifestyle and the back-porch view of their flock and the quiet landscape.

APPENDICES

BUILDING A CHEESE PLATE

Always choose quality over quantity. Your palate has a better chance of keeping up with your appetite if you have a smaller selection rather than a larger one. Pair your choices with a fruity wine, artisan beer or cider, and fruit rather than crackers and bread, which can distract from the cheese flavor.

Variety is the spice of life. Select at least three cheeses and not more than six to sample. Unless you are interested in focusing on one particular type of milk, mix up the offering a bit with a cow's milk, goat's milk, sheep's milk, mixed milk, or buffalo-milk cheeses.

Mix up the cheese styles and textures. For a cheese course, try a fresh-ripened chèvre; a soft, bloomy-rind cow's milk cheese; a semisoft, washed-rind sheep's milk cheese; a hard, cave-aged cow's milk cheese; and a mixed-milk blue cheese. Be sure to place the label next to the cheese for reference, and get to know your favorites.

CHEESE PAIRING SUGGESTIONS

COW CHEESE (SPECIFICALLY CHEDDAR)

Wine: Robust and dry red wine, such as Tempranillo from the Rioja region of Spain

Beer: Brown, dark English ale or Guinness

GOAT CHEESE

Wine: Lighter style red such a Beaujolais, the Moristel grape varietal from Spain, or the Rhône varietal Grenache Blanc, any of which will pick up the herbal qualities of the goat's milk

Beer: Light, fruity ale

SHEEP CHEESE

Wine: Italian Greco di Tufo white wine or Pinot Noir

Beer: Medium-body English ale, such as St. Peters

See page 9 for detailed descriptions of the following specific cheese types.

FRESH, UNRIPENED CHEESES

Food: Think savory and sweet—pair with honey, berry jams, or fresh fruit, such as grapes and peaches.

Beverages: Serve with a Rhône varietal such as a Viognier or Roussanne, or with an Italian Vermentino.

An assortment of Jasper Hill Farm cheese includes soft ripened, semi-soft blue cheese and washed rind hard cheese. Photo courtesy of Jasper Hill Farm.

FRESH, RIPENED CHEESES

Food: Serve with something light and tart or with fresh fruit such as grapes, apricots, berries, and fresh figs.

Beverages: Pair with a rosé or light beer or with a light red wine such as Beaujolais.

SOFT, MOLD-RIPENED CHEESES

Food: Think juicy and acidic to offset the buttery nature and strong flavor of the cheese; serve with sourdough baguettes, walnut-rye bread, plums, or cranberry chutney.

Beverages: Combine with a German-style beer called Hefeweizen, which has lemony tones, or an India pale ale (IPA). For wine, try an Alsatian Pinot Gris, Pinot Blanc, or Old World–style Chardonnay.

SEMISOFT CHEESES

Food: Mildly flavored, semisoft cheeses are ideal for packing in picnics, as they stay neat, or for melting into a kid-friendly cheese sandwich. Serve with tomatoes, pickled onions, or slices of tart apple.

Beverages: For wine, try Beaujolais or a light Spanish red; for beer, try a good brown ale.

HARD CHEESES

Food: Grate over pasta. Serve with thinly sliced tart apples, pears, or other fall-harvested fruit. Serve with fig and thick fruit spreads and with olives or tapenade.

Beverages: Combines well with red Italian wine such as a Chianti or a Rosso di Montepulciano. For beer, try a dark, hearty ale.

WASHED- OR BRUSHED-RIND CHEESES

Food: Similar to hard cheese, these demand an aromatic accompaniment. Serve with mustard on fennel and pepper crackers or alongside sliced prosciutto, pickles, caramelized onions, and fig tapenade.

Beverages: Pair with a heavier Italian or Spanish red wine, or check out a hard cider or dark ale such as Guinness.

BLUE CHEESES

Food: Balance the strong flavor with sweet dates, figs, honey, dates, and walnuts. Ideal for arugula salads and with chunks of cooked beets.

Beverages: Combine with a tawny Port, Shiraz, or a rich white wine, such as Gewurztraminer.

HOW TO WRAP
AND STORE CHEESE

CHEESE IS A LIVING FOOD, and it needs to breathe. When you buy fresh soft cheese, it is often wrapped in a lined paper that is imported from France and designed to help cheese to breathe and continue to ripen. A clean wrap of this paper each time you open your cheese is ideal; however, waxed paper, parchment paper, or butcher paper will work reasonably well. It's best not to store cheese wrapped tightly in plastic wrap, because the plastic suffocates the cheese and can impart an unpleasant chemical odor.

Depending on the cheese and the condition of your refrigerator (humid or dry), you may want to cover the waxed-paper-wrapped cheese with plastic wrap to preserve moisture and keep the flavor intact. Avoid bringing the plastic wrap in contact with the cheese. Soft cheese can be stored in a plastic container for up to a week. Store your cheese in an area of higher humidity such as the meat or vegetable drawer, and keep a thermometer nearby to be sure that the temperature registers close to 45 degrees.

Many cave-aged cheeses have an unusual rind. Should you eat the rind? The flavor is more concentrated near the rind, so first enjoy the center of the cheese. Then, if you like, go ahead and eat the rind. The rind is the skin of the cheese and can sometimes be bitter, yet it is always completely edible.

While it is best to savor fresh cheese right away, most cheese will keep for several days to several weeks if properly stored. Aged, hard cheeses will last longer than fresh, soft ones. Any cheese will grow white, blue, yellow, or black mold over time. These molds are natural and harmless, but can add unwanted sharpness or bitterness to the flavor. So scraping the mold from the surface of the cheese is recommended. Keep blue cheese away from other cheese and wrap it more tightly, as the blue mold will spread.

Before serving cheese, expose it to room-temperature air for at least 30 minutes to allow the natural flavor to truly shine.

SHELF LIFE

The life of cheese depends on its type and what stage of development it was in when you bought it. Hopefully, the cheese you purchase has been marked with the date it was made or with the desirable shelf life. Here is generally how long different types of cheese will last once they have been cut from the main wheel and exposed to the typical home refrigerator, which can fluctuate radically in moisture and temperature.

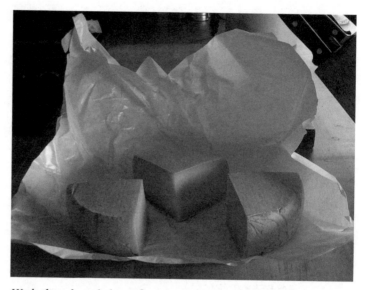

Washed rind aged cheese from Dancing Cow will keep developing flavor if kept in proper wrapping paper and maintained at optimum temperatures.

Fresh: 7 days

Bloomy-rind: 10 to 12 days

Semisoft: 14 days

Washed-rind: 14 to 20 days

Blue: 10 to 14 days (In order to keep mold contained, be sure to wrap blue cheese tightly and keep it separate from other cheeses.)

TASTING NOTES WORKSHEET

HERE ARE A FEW SUGGESTIONS for how to set up a framework for tasting and evaluating as you travel the Vermont Cheese Trail. It will help you keep track of your new discoveries and build a collection of favorites. Be sure to save the cheese label for future reference.

CHEESE NAME: _____

DATE PURCHASED: _____

CHEESEMAKER: _____

COUNTY/REGION: _____

MILK SOURCE:　Cow　　Goat　　Sheep　　Combination

CHEESE TYPE:_____

SHAPE:　Flat　　Pryamid　　Round　　Square　　Wedge　　Cut from a wheel
　　　　　Container

RIND APPEARANCE:　Bloomy　　Natural　　Waxed　　Moldy

AROMA:　Milky　　Floral　　Fruity　　Nutty　　Toasted　　Caramel　　Spicy

FLAVOR:　Milky　　Floral　　Buttery　　Sweet or Honeylike　　Mushroomy　　Smokey
　　　　　Citrusy　　Clovelike　　Salty　　Strong　　Mild

SERVED WITH: _____

REFLECTIONS: _____

_____

_____

FINAL RATING:　Amazing　　Very Good　　Moderate

CHEESE-TASTING DESCRIPTIONS

COLORS
Creamy
Bloomy
Bone
Blue veined
Off white
Pinkish
White
Yellow

SHAPE
Flat
Pyramid
Round
Square
Tall cylinder
Wedge

RIND CHARACTERISTICS
Bandage-wrapped
Bloomy
Crinkled
Greasy
Herb-crusted
Moldy
Moist
Mottled
Natural
Thick
Thin
Washed
Waxed

AROMA
Animal-like
Floral
Fruity
Milky
Nutty
Spicy
Toasty
Vegetablelike

MOUTH FEEL
Chalky
Cracking
Crumbly
Flaky
Grainy
Rough
Rubbery
Runny
Smooth
Spongy
Springy

FLAVOR
Acidic
Barnyard-flavored
Beefy
Biting
Bitter
Bland
Buttery
Caramelized
Citrusy
Clove-flavored
Complex
Floral
Fresh
Fruity
Goaty
Hay-flavored
Honey-flavored
Metallic
Moldy
Musty
Nutmeg-flavored
Nutty
Oily
Rancid
Robust
Roasted vegetable
Salty
Savory
Sharp
Smoky
Sour
Spicy
Sweet
Tangy
Woodsy
Zesty

FOR CHEDDAR CHEESE
Brothy
Fruity
Milky
Nutty

FOR FRESH GOAT CHEESE
Citrusy
Coconutty
Grape-flavored
Green
Honey-flavored
Mushroomy

CHEESEMAKING CLASSES

LEARNING HOW TO MAKE CHEESE is one of the best ways to truly appreciate the nuances of the art and science that go into an excellent cheese. In Vermont, there are several opportunities for you to go beyond simply savoring the cheese and explore the world of cheese through a cheesemaking workshop. Some Vermont cheesemakers welcome visitors to their farms during the slower months (in fall and winter) for cheesemaking classes, and it's worth inquiring at a nearby farm. Or you can check out classes held at either one of these resources:

1. VERMONT INSTITUTE FOR ARTISAN CHEESE

University of Vermont
255 Marsh Life Science Building
109 Carrigan Drive
Burlington, VT 05405
(802) 656-8300
www.uvm.edu/~viac/

The range of topics offered by this unique institute, headquartered at the University of Vermont campus, is designed for individuals considering cheesemaking as a career or for established cheesemakers seeking to increase their knowledge. But all levels of cheesemakers are welcome. Classes are taught by professional faculty and staff and cover the essential principles of cheesemaking (three-day course), basic sensory evaluation (one-day course), milk chemistry (one-day course), and hygiene and food safety (two-day course).

2. PETER DIXON, DAIRY FOODS CONSULTING

P.O. Box 993
Putney, VT 05346
(802) 387-4041
info@dairyfoodsconsulting.com

Each year, experienced cheesemaker and private consultant Peter Dixon teaches a series of two-day workshops for farmstead and artisan cheesemakers using goat, cow, and sheep milk. The workshops are conducted at Woodcock Sheep Cheese Farm in Weston, Taylor Farm in Londonderry, and Consider Bardwell Farm in West Pawlet. Through hands-on lessons, participants learn the fundamentals of farmstead cheesemaking and how to set up and improve their own farmstead cheese businesses. There is a strong focus on the technical aspects of cheesemaking and affinage as well as information on facilities, equipment, marketing, and operations.

3. THE VERMONT CHEESE COUNCIL

2083 East Main Street
Richmond, VT 05477
1-866-261-8595
www.vtcheese.com

The Vermont Cheese Council is a not-for-profit organization, dedicated to promoting high quality cheese, and providing the community of Vermont cheesemakers with technical assistance to continually improve their cheeses.

Some of the Vermont cheesemakers offer classes on their farms during the slower winter months. To visit cheesemakers on their farms, and to find out more about how cheese is made, follow the Vermont Cheese Trail found on the Web site and printed brochures available at Vermont welcome centers or by calling the number listed above.

TECHNICAL TERMS
AND PHRASES

*Here are some technical terms and phrases that will guide you in your quest for
cheese knowledge and help you navigate the world of farmstead and artisan cheese.*

ASH: Otherwise known as cendre, this dark vegetable ash is sprinkled on cheese—most often goat's milk cheese.

AFFINAGE: The craft of maturing and aging cheeses. Often involves frequently turning the cheese and cultivating healthy molds in a temperature-controlled environment.

AFFINEUR/AFFINEUSE: The person behind the affinage or maturation and aging of cheeses.

ARTISAN: A skilled manual craftsperson.

ARTISANAL CHEESE: Cheese that has been handcrafted in small batches according to time-honored techniques, recipes, and traditions. Often made from milk not produced at the farm where the cheesemaking takes place.

BLOOMY RIND: A rind that ripens from the outside in. Soft-ripened cheeses, such as Camembert and Brie, have a bloomy rind.

BLUING: The blue mold found in blue cheeses. Introduced in the cheesemaking process and encouraged to grow during the affinage.

BRINE: A water-and-salt mixture or some type of acidic liquid used to "wash" cheeses prior to affinage. Encourages healthy microflora and promotes flavor development.

BUTTERFAT CONTENT: The amount of fat in cheese or milk. Butterfat content will vary from animal breed and type and affect the cheese recipe and final flavor of the cheese.

CALF RENNET: A substance derived from rennin, an enzyme found in the fourth stomach of a milk-fed calf. Used to coagulate (curdle) milk. Authentic rennet has largely been replaced with synthetic or vegetable-based sources.

CASEIN: The technical name for milk protein. Casein is broken in half by rennet in the production of cheese, forming curds and whey.

CAVE: Originally a real cave or a cellar that provides naturally derived spores and microflora to help ripen the cheese. Today, the term usually means a specially calibrated refrigerated cooler used to maintain the precise humidity and temperature levels ideal for aging cheese.

CHEESECLOTH: A cotton cloth with fine holes. Used to drain cheese curds or line cheese molds. Sometimes called bandage or gauze.

CHÈVRE: A cheese made from goat's milk.

CURD: The solid portion of coagulated or curdled milk, critical to the cheesemaking process.

CURING: The stage in cheesemaking when the cheese is left to ripen and will lose some of its moisture. Also known as ripening, affinage, or aging.

DRAINING: The process by which liquid whey is separated from solid curds. The length of this process will vary according to various cheese types and desired results.

ENZYMES: Proteins that naturally enhance the coagulation of milk, along with rennet.

EYES: The technical name for holes created by a gas introduced during the early cheesemaking stages of certain cheeses (such as Swiss cheese).

FARMSTEAD CHEESE: Cheese made from milk produced on the same farm where the cheese is produced.

FRESH CHEESE: Cheese that has not been ripened or aged; usually made from pasteurized milk.

FRESHEN: Breeding a female animal in order to get the milk she produces for her young. When a female dairy animal gives birth, she lets down milk for her newborn to begin to nurse. Most farmers and cheesemakers will allow the young animals to milk for the first few weeks, but then transfer them to bottle-feeding.

HARD CHEESE: Cheese that has been pressed, causing it to lose moisture, and then aged for a minimum of three months to develop a firm texture and complex flavor.

LACTIC ACID: The acid produced in milk or curds during cheesemaking, as a result of adding a bacterial starter culture.

LACTOSE: The natural sugar found in milk.

MOLDING: A step in the cheesemaking process in which curds are poured into a form—usually made from metal, cloth, or plastic—that is lined in cheesecloth and contains holes to allow for drainage. These molds help determine the final shape of the cheese.

NATURAL-RIND CHEESE: Once the cheese is ready to be aged or ripened, it can be waxed or left with a natural rind, or crust, to protect the interior of the cheese. Many of the natural-rind cheeses will develop beneficial and harmless molds that will ripen the cheese and enhance the flavor.

PASTEURIZATION: The process of heating milk to destroy bacteria, rendering the milk "clean." The typical pasteurization method is HTST—*h*igh *t*emperature, *s*hort *t*ime—in which milk is held at a temperature of 161.5 degrees for at least fifteen seconds.

PENICILLIUM CANDIDUM: A mold often added as a starter culture to soft-ripened cheeses to promote the growth of a white, bloomy rind.

PRESSING: Applying pressure to drained curds to expel additional excess moisture and whey. The amount of pressure that is used will largely depend on the type of cheese; for instance, hard cheeses are pressed more firmly than softer cheeses.

PIERCING: Using long needles to open air passages in blue cheese and so encourage blue mold growth.

RAW MILK: Milk that has been heated, but not to high enough temperatures to be pasteurized.

RENNET: A substance used to coagulate the milk of some types of cheese. Traditionally derived from the lining of the fourth stomach of an unweaned ruminant animal (a calf, kid, or lamb), rennet today is made from fungal, bacterial, or vegetative sources rather than from livestock. It is highly concentrated and only a very small amount is used.

RIND: The outside of a cheese. Acts as a barrier between the cheese and the outside environment, while also imparting a flavor of its own.

SALTING: Adding salt to draw out liquid, enhance flavors, and stave off pathogenic bacteria. Salt is most often sprinkled over the curds before pressing. Different types of cheese require salting at different stages of the production process.

SOFT CHEESE: Unpressed, high-moisture cheese that is aged for relatively short periods. Camembert and Brie are popular examples of soft cheese.

SOFT-RIPENED CHEESE: Cheese with a specific mold culture added to the milk or misted onto the finished cheese to produce a soft rind that will ripen the cheese from the outside in. Brie and Camembert cheese styles fall into this category. These cheeses are usually made from pasteurized milk, since they will be sold young.

STARTER CULTURE: Bacteria, usually *Streptococci* and *Lactobacilli*, added to milk at the very beginning of the cheesemaking process to change the lactose of the milk to lactic acid, speed coagulation, and add to the complexity of flavor of the finished cheese.

TANGY: A characteristic typical of goat's milk cheese. Cheeses that are higher in acid often have a tangy flavor.

TERROIR: An inimitable combination of soil, climate, and geography that enhances the flavor of food. In the case of cheese, this essence is derived from the animals' milk and the affinage, especially if the cheese is aged on premises in an underground cave.

TOMME: The French word for a wheel of cheese that is made from local milk of either cow, goat, sheep or a combination. A tomme is typically made from uncooked milk and weighs between 8–10 pounds, with a natural rind, and is aged between 3–9 months. A tomme can also be any medium-sized wheel or a specific type of cheese.

UNPASTEURIZED CHEESE: Cheese made from raw milk. U.S. regulations require unpasteurized or raw-milk cheese must be aged at least sixty days before it can be sold.

VEGETARIAN RENNET: Rennet made from vegetable sources, such as the cardoon thistle plant, instead of animals.

WASHED-RIND CHEESE: An aged cheese that is brushed with salty water, brine, cider, beer, spirits, or wine to promote healthy mold and develop flavor.

WAX: Wax or paraffin is used to coat cheeses to protect it during transport and to discourage mold growth on the surface while it ages.

WHEY: The liquid portion of the milk left when milk is curdled. High in protein and carbohydrates, it is often fed back to livestock or spread on fields and gardens for fertilizer.

INDEX